T0021806

EASTERN ORTHODOX CHRISTIANS FROM GEORGIA (COUNTRY)

Zviad Gamsakhurdia, Eduard Shevardnadze, Ilia Chavchavadze, Patriarch Ilia Ii of Georgia, Grigol Peradze, Besarion Jughashvili, Anthim the Iberian, Ketevan of Kakheti, Patriarch Kyrion Ii of Georgia, Ekvtime Takaishvili, Tornikios, Luarsab Ii of Kartli, Ketevan Geladze, Lasha Zhvania

BOOKS LLC

Publication Data:

Title: Eastern Orthodox Christians From Georgia (Country)

Subtitle: Zviad Gamsakhurdia, Eduard Shevardnadze, Ilia Chavchavadze, Patriarch Ilia Ii of Georgia, Grigol Peradze, Besarion Jughashvili, Anthim the Iberian, Ketevan of Kakheti, Patriarch Kyrion Ii of Georgia, Ekvtime Takaishvili, Tornikios, Luarsab Ii of Kartli, Ketevan Geladze, Lasha Zhvania

Published by: Books LLC, Memphis, Tennessee, USA in 2010

Copyright (chapters): http://creativecommons.org/licenses/by-sa/3.0

Online edition: http://booksllc.net/?q=Category:Eastern_Orthodox_Christians_from_Georgia_(country)

Contact the publisher: http://booksllc.net/contactus.cfm

CONTENTS

Introduction	v
Anthim the Iberian	1
Besarion Jughashvili	5
Constantin Andronikof	9
Eduard Shevardnadze	11
Ekvtime Takaishvili	19
Elie Melia	21
Grigol Peradze	23
Ilia Chavchavadze	27
Ketevan Geladze	33
Ketevan of Kakheti	35
Lasha Zhvania	39
Luarsab II of Kartli	41
Patriarch Callistratus of Georgia	43
Patriarch Christophorus III of Georgia	45

Patriarch David V of Georgia   47
Patriarch Ephraim II of Georgia   49
Patriarch Ilia II of Georgia   51
Patriarch Kyrion II of Georgia   55
Patriarch Leonid of Georgia   59
Patriarch Melchizedek III of Georgia   61
Tornikios   63
Zviad Gamsakhurdia   65

Index   79

Introduction

The online edition of this book is at http://booksllc.net/?q=Category:Eastern%
5FOrthodox%5FChristians%5Ffrom%5FGeorgia%5F%28country%29. It's hyperlinked and may be updated. Where we have recommended related pages, you can
read them at http://booksllc.net/?q= followed by the page's title. Most entries in the
book's index also have a dedicated page at http://booksllc.net/?q= followed by the
index entry.

Each chapter in this book ends with a URL to a hyperlinked online version. Use the
online version to access related pages, websites, footnote URLs. You can click the
history tab on the online version to see a list of the chapter's contributors. While we
have included photo captions in the book, due to copyright restrictions you can only
view the photos online. You also need to go to the online edition to view some formula
symbols.

The online version of this book is part of Wikipedia, a multilingual, web-based
encyclopedia.

Wikipedia is written collaboratively. Since its creation in 2001, Wikipedia has grown
rapidly into one of the largest reference web sites, attracting nearly 68 million visitors

monthly. There are more than 91,000 active contributors working on more than 15 million articles in more than 270 languages. Every day, hundreds of thousands of active from around the world collectively make tens of thousands of edits and create thousands of new articles.

After a long process of discussion, debate, and argument, articles gradually take on a neutral point of view reached through consensus. Additional editors expand and contribute to articles and strive to achieve balance and comprehensive coverage. Wikipedia's intent is to cover existing knowledge which is verifiable from other sources. The ideal Wikipedia article is well-written, balanced, neutral, and encyclopedic, containing comprehensive, notable, verifiable knowledge.

Wikipedia is open to a large contributor base, drawing a large number of editors from diverse backgrounds. This allows Wikipedia to significantly reduce regional and cultural bias found in many other publications, and makes it very difficult for any group to censor and impose bias. A large, diverse editor base also provides access and breadth on subject matter that is otherwise inaccessible or little documented.

Think you can improve the book? If so, simply go to the online version and suggest changes. If accepted, your additions could appear in the next edition!

ANTHIM THE IBERIAN

St. Anthim the Iberian (Antim Ivireanul)

- ○ Born: c. 1650, Georgia
- ○ Died: 1716, Adrianopol
- ○ Venerated in: Romanian Orthodox Church
- ○ Canonized: 1992-09-27, Bucharest by the Synod of the Romanian Orthodox Church
- ○ Feast: 27 September (NS)

Online image: Anthim's coat of arms in an 18th century manuscript

Anthim the Iberian (Romanian: *Antim Ivireanul*, Georgian: - *Antimoz Iverieli*; secular name: *Andria*; 1650 September or October 1716) was one of the greatest ecclesiastic figures of Wallachia (and, through modern extension, Romania), a noted Eastern Orthodox theologian and philosopher, founder of the first printing press in Romania, and Metropolitan of Bucharest in 1708-1715.

Biography

He was an ethnic Georgian born in Caucasian Iberia (Kartli, nowadays in the Republic of Georgia). Anthim was taken prisoner by Ottoman Empire troops, and took orders in Istanbul, while living on the compounds of the Ecumenical Patriarchate of Constantinople. In 1689 or 1690, he was asked to settle in Wallachia by Prince Constantin Brâncoveanu, and was given charge of the newly-founded princely printing press in Bucharest. Being appointed father superior (*egumen*) of the Snagov Monastery, Anthim moved the press to the new location.

He became bishop of Râmnicu in 1705, and in 1708 Metropolitan of Wallachia. Anthim spoke and wrote many Oriental and European languages. Although a foreigner, he soon acquired a thorough knowledge of Romanian, and was instrumental in helping to introduce that language into the local church as its official language. In 1693, he published the *Gospels* in Romanian.

In 1709 Anthim was a founder of the first Georgian printing press in Tbilisi; he also trained Georgians in the art of printing, and cut the type with which under his pupil Mihail Ishtvanovitch they printed the first of Georgian *Gospels* (1710). In addition, Anthim published 25 other books - in Romanian, as well as Church Slavonic, Greek, and Arabic (usually in bilingual volumes, such as the Greek-Arabic *Missal* of 1702); this meant that he was also the first in Wallachia to use Arabic fonts).

His personal work, *Didahiile*, was a collection of sermons meant as a sharp critique of contemporary habits and morals; notably, beside Christian sources, Anthim made reference to classical philosophy. Alongside his literary output, the cleric was the builder of the *All-Saints Monastery* in Bucharest - nowadays known as the Antim Monastery in his memory.

Anthim's overt opposition to Ottoman tutelage over Wallachia made him an adversary of the Phanariote regime. The new Prince Nicholas Mavrocordatos imprisoned him, and subsequently exiled him to Mount Sinai. Anthim was captured by the Ottomans while he was taking the trip, and assassinated somewhere in modern-day Bulgaria (his body would have been discarded in the Maritsa or the Tundzha). It is alleged that his murder was ordered by Mavrocordatos himself.

In 1992 Anthim was canonized by the Romanian Orthodox Church. A rugby union trophy, contested by Romania and Georgia is named after him - the *Antim Cup*.

References (URLs online)

- *This article incorporates text from the* Encyclopædia Britannica, *Eleventh Edition, a publication now in the public domain. In turn, it cites as references:*
  - M. Gaster, *Chrestomathie roumaine* (1881) and "Gesch. d. rumänischen Litteratur," in Grober, *Grundriss d. rom. Philologie*, vol. ii. (1899)
  - E. Picot, *Notice sur Anthim d'Ivir* (Paris, 1886).

o "Anthimus of Iberia", in *Encyclopædia Britannica*, 2007 edition.   Retrieved May 23, 2007, from Encyclopædia Britannica Online
o "Antimoz Iverieli", in *Sakartvelo Encyclopedia*, Vol. I, Tbilisi, 1997, p.158
o Otar Gvinchidze, *Antimoz Iverieli*, Tbilisi, 1973

Websites (URLs online)

o (Romanian) *Didahii* (online transcript)

A hyperlinked version of this chapter is at http://booksllc.net?q=Anthim%5Fthe%5FIberian

BESARION JUGHASHVILI

Besarion Vanovis Jughashvili

- o Born: ca. 1850 Gori, Didi Lilo, Russian Empire
- o Died: August 25, 1909 Tbilisi, Russian Empire
- o Occupation: cobbler
- o Spouse(s): Ketevan Geladze
- o Children: Mikheil Giorgi Joseph Stalin
- o Parents: Vano Djughashvili

Besarion Vanovis Jughashvili (Georgian: ; Russian: ;) (born ca. 1850 August 25, 1909) was Joseph Stalin's father. His surname means *son of Juga*, and is derived from either the Ossetian *Juga* (that means 'herd') or the old Georgian *djogi* - 'steel'.[1]

Family and early life

Besarion Jughashvili was the grandson of Zaza Jughashvili from the village of Geri, north of Gori. In the mid-19th century, Zaza took part in a peasant uprising in Ananuri, a small county seat near Ger on the Aragva River. The uprising was crushed by Tsarist soldiers, and Zaza was captured with nine other rebels. Zaza escaped and hid in Gori, where he was recaptured and remanded as a serf to Prince Eristavi. He became involved in another uprising on the Eristavi estate. It is unknown who his wife was, or the exact number of children he sired.[2] Vano Djughashvili, Besarion's father, tended the vineyards of Georgian Prince Badur Machabeli in the village of Didi-Lilo. Besarion is known to have been born into an Orthodox Christian serf family from the village of Didi Lilo in Georgia, most likely in 1850. Besarion had a brother called Georgy who was murdered by bandits.[1]

Later life and Stalin

According to the Arsoshvili family (Djughashvili's relatives and longtime residents of Didi Lilo), Djughashvili couldn't afford paying a three-ruble tax and had to move to Gori in search of employment.[1]

Online image: Besarion Jughashvili's grave in Telavi, Georgia.

In Gori, he lived in a house of Kulumbegashvili. Here, Jughashvili found a job as a cobbler and married Ekaterina (Keke) Geladze on May 30 1872. He was known as a polyglot, being fluent in Georgian, Russian, Turkish and Armenian.[1] It is known that their first two children (Mikhail and Giorgy) died as infants. Beso soon developed a severe drinking problem. Stalin's French biographer Souvarine speculated that Stalin's birth defects, notably his adjoining two toes, were probably due to his father's alcoholism.[3] Djughashvili eventually opened his own workshop, and for a time he and his family were prosperous and happy, until his drinking problem resurfaced. He subsequently became very abusive toward his wife and son, at one point having tried to strangle Keke.[1] His ability to work also suffered, to the point that his workshop was kept alive only by his apprentices. Although Besarion wanted his son to follow in his footsteps and become a cobbler, his mother instead had Joseph enrolled in school to be educated for the Orthodox priesthood. This enraged Besarion; in a drunken rage, he vandalized a local tavern and attacked the village police chief. For this he was expelled from Gori. He moved to Tbilisi, where he found work at the Adelkhanov Shoe Factory, whilst his wife and son stayed in Gori. When his son entered an Orthodox seminary in Tbilisi, Beso made an unsuccessful attempt to remove him and teach him the cobbler's trade instead. After Stalin was expelled from the seminary, Beso met his son for the last time. Soso, as he was called, was attempting to organize a strike in the factory where Beso worked. Beso contemptuously told his son that he would have done better to learn a trade.[1]

Besarion died on August 25, 1909 in Mikhailovsky Hospital in Tiflis, suffering from tuberculosis, colitis and chronic pneumonia.[1] He is buried in Telavi, Georgia.

References (URLs online)

   o 1. Simon Sebag Montefiore. Young Stalin. 2007. ISBN 978-0-297-85068-7

o 2. Edward Ellis Smith, *The Young Stalin: the early years of an elusive revolutionary*, cassell & company LTD. 1968
o 3. Leon Trotsky, *Stalin: An appraisal of the man and his influence*, edited and translated from the Russian by Charles Malamuth, London: Hollis and Carter, LTD. 1947

Further reading

o Simon Sebag Montefiore: *Young Stalin*, 2007

A hyperlinked version of this chapter is at http://booksllc.net?q=Besarion%5FJughashvili

3

CONSTANTIN ANDRONIKOF

Prince **Constantin Andronikof** (Russian: , *Konstantin Eseevich Andronikov*; Georgian: , *Konstantine Andronikashvili*) (July 16, 1916 September 12, 1997) was a French diplomat, religious writer and translator.

He was born in a notable Georgian aristocratic family of Andronikashvili in St. Petersburg, Imperial Russia. During the Russian Civil War in 1920, he, in the arms of his mother, fled to France, while his father was arrested by the Bolsheviks and later shot during the Great Purge of 1937.

Constantin Andronilof graduated from the University of Paris in 1940 and St. Sergius Orthodox Theological Institute (of which he subsequently became professor) in 1944. He later worked for the French Ministry of Foreign Affairs and served as an English and Russian interpreter to President de Gaulle.

Andronikof became best known as the most prolific French translator of Russian religious thought, especially of the theological works by Fr. Sergei Bulgakov. From

1991 to 1993, he served as a dean of St. Sergius Orthodox Theological Institute in Paris.[1]

Works

- Le sens des fetes: T. 1. Le cycle fixe. Paris: Cerf, 1970. 309 p.
- Les Notes apologetiques.
- Le sens des fetes: T. 2. Le cycle pascal. Lausanne: L'age d'homme, 1985.
- Le sens de la Liturgie: La relation entre Dieu et l'homme. Paris: Cerf, 1988. 322 p.

References (URLs online)

- 1.
    - : , , : 1921 1972 / . . .- Boston: G. K. Hall & Co., 1973.
    - L'Oreille du Logos: In memoriam Constantin Andronikof. Lausanne: L'age d'homme, 1999. . 94-100.
    - . . XX . .: ; , 2001. . 42-44.
  All cited at (Russian)

A hyperlinked version of this chapter is at http://booksllc.net?q=Constantin%5FAndronikof

4

EDUARD SHEVARDNADZE

Eduard Shevardnadze

- o 2nd President of Georgia
- o **In office** 23 November 1995 23 November 2003
- o Preceded by: Zviad Gamsakhurdia
- o Succeeded by: Nino Burjanadze (acting)
- o Foreign Minister of the Soviet Union
- o **In office** 27 July 1985 20 December 1990
- o Preceded by: Andrei Gromyko
- o Succeeded by: Aleksandr Bessmertnykh
- o **In office** 19 November 1991 26 December 1991
- o Preceded by: Boris Pankin
- o Succeeded by: Andrey Kozyrev (as Foreign Minister of the Russian Federation)
- o Born: 25 January 1928 (1928-01-25) Mamati, Guria, Transcaucasian SFSR, Soviet Union
- o Nationality: Georgian
- o Political party: Union of Citizens of Georgia, formerly CPSU
- o Spouse(s): Nanuli Shevardnadze

Eduard Shevardnadze (Georgian: , IPA: [du rd v rdn dz]; Russian: , *Eduard Amvrosiyevich Shevardnadze*; born 25 January 1927 / 28 is written in papers) served as the second President of Georgia from 1995 until he resigned on 23 November 2003 as a consequence of the bloodless Rose Revolution. Prior to his presidency, he served under Mikhail Gorbachev as the Minister of Foreign Affairs of the Soviet Union from 1985 to 1991. Shevardnadze's political skills earned him the nickname of *tetri melia* (white fox).

Early life and family

Shevardnadze was born in Mamati, Lanchkhuti, Transcaucasian SFSR, Soviet Union. His father, a teacher, was very poor; he had a sister and three brothers, one of whom was killed in World War II. In 1937, during the Great Purge, his father, who had abandoned Menshevism for Bolshevism in the mid-1920s, was arrested but was released due to the intervention of an NKVD officer who had been his pupil.[1] In 1951, Shevardnadze married Nanuli Tsagareishvili in a move he had been warned might wreck his career (her father had been executed as an "enemy of the people"); she died on 20 October 2004.

Career

He joined the Communist Party of the Soviet Union in 1948 after two years as a Komsomol instructor and rose through the ranks to become a member of the Georgian Supreme Soviet in 1959. He was appointed Georgian Minister for the maintenance of public order in 1965 and subsequently became Georgian Minister for Internal Affairs from 1968 to 1972 with the rank of general in the police. He was appointed as General Secretary of the Georgian Communist Party by the Kremlin with the task of suppressing the grey and black-market capitalism that was growing in defiance of structure of the state and purge the local party ranks.[2]

Shevardnadze gained a reputation as a fierce opponent of corruption, which was endemic in the republic, dismissing and imprisoning hundreds of officials. One of his first reported acts was to call for a show of hands by senior officials and promptly ordering all those displaying expensive black-market watches to take them off and hand them in. However, he never succeeded in entirely stamping out corruption. As late as 1980, he found it necessary to reiterate that economic and social development depended on "an uncompromising struggle against such negative phenomena as money-grabbing, bribe-taking, misappropriation of socialist property, private-property tendencies, theft and other deviations from the norms of communist morality."

- Communist Party of the Soviet Union
- **History**
- Organization
- Congress · Central Committee Politburo · General Secretary Secretariat · Orgburo Control Committee Auditing Commission

- Leaders
- Vladimir Lenin Joseph Stalin Nikita Khrushchev Leonid Brezhnev Yuri Andropov Konstantin Chernenko Mikhail Gorbachev
- Other topics
- *Pravda* Komsomol
- Communism portal
-

A corruption scandal in 1972 forced the resignation of Vasily Mzhavanadze, the First Secretary of the Georgian Communist Party. His downfall may have been precipitated by Shevardnadze, who was the natural replacement candidate and was duly appointed to the post. During his time as First Secretary, he continued to attack corruption and dealt firmly with dissidents. In 1977, as part of a Soviet Union-wide sweep against human rights activists, his government imprisoned a number of prominent Georgian dissidents on the grounds of anti-Soviet activities. These included the leading dissidents Merab Kostava and Zviad Gamsakhurdia, who later became the first democratically elected President of the Republic of Georgia. On the other hand, he managed to gain from the central authorities an unprecedented concession to the 1978 Georgian national movement in defense of the constitutional status of the Georgian language.

Shevardnadze's hard line on corruption soon caught the attention of the Soviet hierarchy. He joined the Central Committee of the Soviet Communist Party in 1976 and in 1978 was promoted to the rank of candidate (non-voting) member of the Soviet Politburo. He remained fairly obscure for a number of years, although he consolidated a reputation for personal austerity, shunning the trappings of high office and travelling to work by public transport rather than using the limousines provided to Politburo members. His chance came in 1985 when the veteran Soviet Minister of Foreign Affairs, Andrei Gromyko, left that post for the largely ceremonial position of Chairman of the Presidium of the Supreme Soviet. The *de facto* leader, Communist Party General Secretary Mikhail Gorbachev, appointed Shevardnadze to replace Gromyko as Minister of Foreign Affairs, thus consolidating Gorbachev's circle of relatively young reformers.

He subsequently played a key role in the détente which marked the end of the Cold War. He was credited with helping to devise the so-called "Sinatra Doctrine" of allowing the Soviet Union's eastern European satellites to "do it their way" rather than forcibly restraining any attempts to pursue a different course. When democratization and revolution began to sweep across eastern Europe, he rejected the pleas of eastern European Communist leaders for Soviet intervention and smoothed the path for a (mostly) peaceful democratic transformation in the region. He reportedly told hardliners that "it is time to realize that neither socialism, nor friendship, nor good-neighborliness, nor respect can be produced by bayonets, tanks or blood." However, his moderation was seen by some communists and Russian nationalists as a betrayal and earned him the long-term antagonism of powerful figures in Moscow.

During the late 1980s, as the Soviet Union descended into crisis, Gorbachev and Shevardnadze became increasingly estranged from each other over policy differences. Gorbachev fought to preserve a socialist government and the unity of the Soviet Union, while Shevardnadze advocated further political and economic liberalisation. He resigned in protest against Gorbachev's policies in December 1990, delivering a dramatic warning to the Soviet parliament that "Reformers have gone and hidden in the bushes. Dictatorship is coming." A few months later, his fears were partially realised when an unsuccessful coup by Communist hardliners precipitated the collapse of the Soviet Union. Shevardnadze returned briefly as Soviet Foreign Minister in November 1991 but resigned with Gorbachev the following month when the Soviet Union was formally dissolved.

In 1991, Shevardnadze was baptized into the Georgian Orthodox Church.[3]

Georgian President

The newly independent Republic of Georgia elected as its first president a leader of the nationalist movement, Zviad Gamsakhurdia, a famous scientist and writer, who had been imprisoned by Shevardnadze's government in the late 1970s. Gamsakhurdia's rule ended abruptly in January 1992 when he was deposed in a bloody coup d'état and forced to flee to the Chechen Republic in neighboring Russia. Shevardnadze was appointed acting chairman of the Georgian state council in March 1992. When the Presidency was restored in November 1995, he was elected with 70% of the vote. He secured a second term in April 2000 in an election that was marred by widespread claims of vote-rigging.

Shevardnadze's career as Georgian President was in some respects even more challenging than his earlier career as Soviet Foreign Minister. He faced many enemies, some dating back to his campaigns against corruption and nationalism in Soviet times. A civil war in western Georgia broke out in 1993 between supporters of Gamsakhurdia and Shevardnadze but was ended by Russian intervention on Shevardnadze's side and the death of ex-President Gamsakhurdia on 31 December 1993. Three assassination attempts were mounted against Shevardnadze. He escaped an assassination attempt in Abkhazia in 1992: Russian military carried out an attack on Shevardnadze's life. Then in August 1995 and February 1998 which his government blamed on remnants of Gamsakhurdia's party. The 1995 attack had seen his motorcade attacked with anti-tank rockets and small arms fire in Tblisi under cover of night.[4]

He also faced separatist conflicts in the regions of South Ossetia and Abkhazia, which caused the deaths of an estimated 10,000 people, as well as an assertively autonomous government in Ajaria.

The war in the Russian republic of Chechnya on Georgia's northern border caused considerable friction with Russia, which accused Shevardnadze of harbouring Chechen guerrillas and supported Georgian separatists in apparent retaliation. Further friction was caused by Shevardnadze's close relationship with the United States, which saw him as a counterbalance to Russian influence in the strategic Transcaucasus region. Under Shevardnadze's strongly pro-Western administration, Georgia became a major recipient of U.S. foreign and military aid, signed a strategic partnership with NATO and declared an ambition to join both NATO and the European Union. Perhaps his greatest diplomatic coup was the securing of a $3 billion project to build a pipeline carrying oil from Azerbaijan to Turkey via Georgia.

At the same time, however, Georgia suffered badly from the effects of crime and rampant corruption, often perpetrated by well-connected officials and politicians. Shevardnadze's closest advisers, including several members of his family, exerted disproportionate economic power. It was estimated by outside observers that Shevardnadze's inner circle controlled as much as 70 per cent of the economy: his wife edited and wrote for one of the country's major newspapers, his daughter was the director of a television film studio and her husband founded one of the country's leading mobile phone networks (with American funding). While Shevardnadze himself was not a conspicuous profiteer, he was accused by many Georgians of shielding corrupt supporters and using his powers of patronage to shore up his own position. Georgia acquired an unenviable reputation as one of the world's most corrupt countries. Eventually, even his American supporters grew tired of pouring money into an apparent black hole.

Political downfall

Online image: Banner on Parliament of Georgia saying: "Georgia without Shevardnadze"

On 2 November 2003, Georgia held a parliamentary election that was widely denounced as unfair by international election observers, as well as by the U.N. and the U.S. government. The outcome sparked fury among many Georgians, leading to mass demonstrations in the capital Tbilisi and elsewhere. Protesters broke into Parliament on 21 November as the first session of the new Parliament was beginning, forcing President Shevardnadze to escape with his bodyguards. He later declared a state of emergency and insisted that he would not resign.

Despite growing tension, both sides publicly stated their wish to avoid any violence, a particular concern given Georgia's turbulent post-Soviet history. Nino Burjanadze, speaker of the Georgian parliament, said she would act as president until the situation was resolved. The leader of the opposition Mikhail Saakashvili stated he would guarantee Shevardnadze's safety and support his return as President provided he promised to call early presidential elections.

On 23 November Shevardnadze met with the opposition leaders Mikheil Saakashvili and Zurab Zhvania to discuss the situation, in a meeting arranged by Russian Foreign Minister Igor Ivanov. After this meeting, the president announced his resignation, declaring that he wished to avert a bloody power struggle "so all this can end peacefully and there is no bloodshed and no casualties". However, it was widely speculated that the refusal of the armed forces to enforce his emergency decree was the main cause of his resignation. He claimed the following day that he had been prepared to step down the previous morning, hours before he actually did, but was prevented from doing so by his entourage.

Although it was unclear precisely what role foreign powers played in the toppling of Shevardnadze, it emerged shortly afterwards that both Russia and the United States had played a direct role. U.S. Secretary of State Colin Powell communicated regularly with Shevardnadze during the post-election crisis, reportedly pushing him to step down peacefully. Russian foreign minister Igor Ivanov flew to Tbilisi to visit three main opposition leaders and Shevardnadze, and arranged on late 23 November for Saakashvili and Zurab Zhvania to meet Shevardnadze. Ivanov then travelled to the autonomous region of Ajaria for consultations with the Ajaran leader Aslan Abashidze, who had been pro-Shevardnadze.

Shevardnadze's ouster prompted mass celebrations with drinking and dancing in the streets by tens of thousands of Georgians crowding Tbilisi's Rustaveli Avenue and Freedom Square. The protesters dubbed their actions a "Rose Revolution", deliberately recalling the peaceful toppling of the Communist government in Czechoslovakia in the "Velvet Revolution" of 1989. Observers noted similarities with the overthrow of Yugoslav President Slobodan Milo evi in 2000, who was also forced to resign by mass protests. The parallel with Yugoslavia was reinforced when it emerged that the Open Society Institute of George Soros had arranged contacts between the Georgian opposition and the Yugoslav Otpor (Resistance) movement, which had been instrumental in the toppling of Milo evi . Otpor activists reportedly advised the Georgian opposition on the methods that they had used to mobilize popular anger against Milo evi . According to the then editor-in-chief of *The Georgian Messenger* newspaper, Zaza Gachechiladze, "It's generally accepted public opinion here that Mr. Soros is the person who planned Shevardnadze's overthrow". IWPR reported that on 28 November, in an interview held with the press at his home, Shevardnadze "spoke with anger" about a plot by "unspecified Western figures" to bring him down. He said that he did not believe that the US administration was involved.

The German government offered Shevardnadze political asylum in Germany, where he is still widely respected for his role as one of the chief Soviet architects of reunification in 1990. It was reported (although never confirmed) that his family had purchased a villa in the resort town of Baden-Baden. However, he told German TV on 24 November, "Although I am very grateful for the invitation from the German side, I love my country very much and I won't leave it." He has begun to write his memoirs following his enforced retirement.

Shevardnadze's legacy

Shevardnadze's political career was filled with contradictions. He was a product of the Soviet system, but played a central role in dismantling that system. He built his reputation on fighting political corruption, but came to be seen as using corrupt methods to shore up his own position. He achieved worldwide renown as the most liberal foreign minister in the history of the USSR, but was never nearly as popular in his own country. He succeeded in maintaining Georgia's territorial integrity in the face of strong separatist pressures, but was unable to restore his government's authority in large areas of the country. He helped to establish a viable civil society in Georgia, but resorted to rigging elections to maintain his powerbase.

When Shevardnadze joined the Georgian state council in 1992 in the chaotic aftermath of the coup against Zviad Gamsakhurdia, he presented himself as being the best candidate to guide Georgia through its difficult rebirth as an independent nation. Over time, he seemed to have become convinced that his interests and those of Georgia were the same, justifying the use of unscrupulous tactics in the apparent belief that Georgia could not survive without him. His downfall ushered in a renewed period of uncertainty in Georgian politics. One positive aspect in the eyes of many observers was the fact that, under his rule, a vigorous civil society had become well established and would possibly be better able to meet the challenge than had been the case in the early 1990s.

Shevardnadze published his memoirs in May 2006 under the title *pikri tsarsulsa da momavalze*, or 'Thoughts about the Past and the Future'. During the 2008 South Ossetia war, he made public his attempts to restore Georgian diplomatic relations with Russia, and continues to argue for it.

References (URLs online)

- 1. Suny, Ronald. *The Making of the Georgian Nation*, pp. 328-9. Indiana University Press, Bloomington, 1994.
- 2. Southern Corruption, *TIME Magazine*, 3 December 1973
- 3. Kolstø, Pål. *Political Construction Sites: Nation-Building in Russia and the Post-Soviet States*, p. 70. Westview Press, Boulder, Colorado, 2000.
- 4. Katz, Samuel M. "Relentless Pursuit: The DSS and the manhunt for the al-Qaeda terrorists", 2002

Bibliography

- Edvard Shevardnadze: As The Iron Curtain Was Torn Down - Encounters And Memories. Metzler, Duisburg 2007 (German: revised, re-designed and expanded edition) [Georgian:"Pikri Tsarsulsa Da Momavalze - Memuarebi", Tbilisi 2006] ISBN 978-3-936283-10-5

- The Future Belongs To Freedom, by Edvard Shevardnadze, translated by Catherine A. Fitzpatrick

External links and sources

- BBC profile
- Foes of Georgian Leader Storm Into Parliament Building by Seth Mydans, from the New York Times Web Site.
- Georgian Interior Minister Vows to Enforce State of Emergency on the Voice of America News Web Site.
- People power forces Georgia leader out from BBC News online.
- MacKinnon, Mark. Georgia revolt carried mark of Soros. *Globe and Mail*, 26 November 2003.
- Russians in Baden-Baden

Party political offices

- Preceded by **Vasil Mzhavanadze**: **First Secretary of the Georgian Communist Party** 1972 1985: Succeeded by **Jumber Patiashvili**
- Political offices
- Preceded by **Andrey Gromyko**: **Foreign Minister of the Soviet Union** 1985 1991: Succeeded by **Aleksandr Bessmertnykh**
- Preceded by **Boris Pankin**: **Foreign Minister of the Soviet Union** 1991: Succeeded by **Andrey Kozyrev, as Foreign Minister of the Russian Federation**
- Preceded by **Zviad Gamsakhurdia**: **President of Georgia** 1995 2003: Succeeded by **Nino Burjanadze**

A hyperlinked version of this chapter is at http://booksllc.net?q=Eduard%5FShevardnadze

5

EKVTIME TAKAISHVILI

Online image: Ekvtime Takaishvili

Online image: Monument in Tbilisi

Ekvtime Takaishvili (also spelled **Taqaishvili**) (Georgian:) (January 3, 1863-February 21, 1953) was a Georgian historian, archaeologist and public benefactor.

Born in the village of Likhauri in the western Georgian province of Guria (then part of Imperial Russia) to a local nobleman Svimon Takaishvili, he graduated from St. Petersburg University in 1887. From 1887 to 1917, he lectured on the history of Georgia at various prestigious schools in Tbilisi, including the Tbilisi Gymnasium for Nobility. During these years, he was actively involved in extensive scholarly activities and chaired, from 1907 to 1921, the Society of History and Ethnography of Georgia. Between 1907 and 1910, he organized a series of archaeological expeditions to the historic Georgian region of Tao-Klarjeti (now part of Turkey).

After the February Revolution, he engaged also in politics, taking part in the estab-
lishment of the National-Democratic Party of Georgia in 1917 and being elected to a
post of Deputy Chairman in the Constituent Assembly of the Democratic Republic of
Georgia from 1919 to 1921.

Georgian national treasury

In 1918, he was among the founders and professors of the Tbilisi State University
(TSU). He lost his tenure both in the parliament and at the TSU in 1921, when
the Bolshevik Russia's 11th Red Army put an end to Georgia's independence. He
followed the Georgian government in their French exile, taking the Georgian national
treasury numerous precious pieces of Georgian material culture - with him to Europe.

The treasury contained into 39 immense boxes, were shipped to Marseille and placed
in a bank depository. Subsequently this precious cargo was transferred to one of the
banks in Paris. Although the treasury was officially the property of the Georgian
government-in-exile, it was actually Ekvtime Takaishvili who supervised this huge
collection. In the early 1930s, Takaishvili won a lawsuit against Salome Obolenskaya
(1878-1961), daughter of the last Mingrelian prince Nikoloz Dadiani, who also laid
claim to a part of the treasury taken from the former Dadiani Palace in Zugdidi,
Georgia. Despite numerous attempts by various European museums to purchase
portions of this treasury, and extreme economic hardship, Takaishvili never sold a
single piece of the priceless collection to live on and guarded it until 1933, when the
League of Nations recognized the Soviet Union; the Georgian embassy in Paris was
abolished and transformed into the "Georgian Office". The treasury passed into the
possession of the French state. In 1935, Takaishvili urged the French government to
hand the collections to Georgia, but it was not until the end of the World War II when
was he able, in November 1944, to attract the attention of the Soviet ambassador A.
Bogomolov to the fate of the Georgian treasury. Joseph Stalin's good relations with
General Charles de Gaulle enabled Takaishvili to bring the treasury back to Georgia.
However, Takaishvili had to spend his long unhappy days in Tbilisi under house arrest,
seemingly considered to be too old to be imprisoned.

He was an author of numerous scholarly works on the history and archaeology of
Georgia and the Caucasus which are of special value even today. In Tbilisi, Tbilisi
Second Gymnasium has been named after him. He has been canonized by the Georgian
Orthodox Church.

References (URLs online)

   o (Georgian) A website dedicated to E. Takaishvili. Retrieved on 2008-07-06.
   o (Russian) , . . - (1917-1991). . . . , ... : , 2003. 496 .

A hyperlinked version of this chapter is at http://booksllc.net?q=Ekvtime%
5FTakaishvili

6

ELIE MELIA

Fr. **Elie Melia** (Georgian:) (February 20, 1915 1988) was a Georgian Orthodox priest and church historian.

Born in Kutaisi, he fled the Soviet regime to Paris where he was closely associated with local Georgian émigré community and later became a priest. He supervised the Georgian parish of St. Nino at Paris, participated in the Russian Student Christian Movement, and taught church history and theology at St. Sergius Orthodox Theological Institute. After World War II, he served at the St. Seraphim of Sarov Church at Colombelle (Normandy).

He is the author and coauthor of several works on Eastern Orthodoxy and the Georgian Orthodox Church.

References (URLs online)

   o (Russian) (Protopope Iliya Melia). *Religious figures and writers of the Russian Abroad.* Accessed on November 20, 2007.

○ (French) LA PAROISSE SAINTE NINO (St. Nino Parish). ASSOCIATION GEORGI-
ENNE EN FRANCE (Georgian Association in France). Accessed on December 19,
2007.

A hyperlinked version of this chapter is at http://booksllc.net?q=Elie%5FMelia

7

GRIGOL PERADZE

Online image: **Grigol Peradze** (*St. Priest Martyr Grigol*), (September 13, 1899 - December 6, 1942) was a famous Georgian ecclesiastic figure, theologian, historian, Archimandrite, PhD of History, Professor.

Life and works

Grigol Peradze was born in the village of Bakurtsikhe, in the Gurjaani district of the Kakheti region, in Eastern Georgia. His father, Romanoz Peradze, was a priest.

In 1918 Peradze graduated from the Tbilisi Theological Seminary, and afterwards studied at the Tbilisi State University until 1921.

On February 25, 1921, Georgia was occupied by Soviet Russia. Grigol Peradze went into exile in Germany in November the same year.

In 1926 he graduated from the University of Bonn (Germany). In 1927 he received a PhD degree in History (the title of his PhD thesis was *"History of the Georgian Monasticism from its creation until 1064"*).

From 1927 - 1932 Peradze was an Associate Professor at the University of Bonn. From 1933 - 1942 he was a Professor of Patrology at the Faculty of Orthodox Theology of Warsaw University, in Poland.

In 1931, Grigol Peradze was ordained a priest in the Greek Orthodox Cathedral of London; in 1934, he received the rank of Archimandrite. In 1931, he founded a Georgian St. Nino Orthodox church in Paris. In the same year he began to publish a Georgian scientific journal titled *"Jvari Vazisa"* ("Cross of Vine").

In the 1930s, Peradze discovered numerous important written manuscripts of Georgian Christian culture in Romania, Bulgaria, Greece, Italy, Germany, and Austria (Georgian manuscripts of the Typicon of the Georgian Petritsoni Monastery (Bachkovo, Bulgaria), the so-called Tischendorf manuscripts of the Apagae of the Monastery of the Holy Cross at the University Library in the University of Leipzig, Germany, etc.).

The invasion of Poland by German troops in 1939 made Peradze's position precarious. For him being in solidarity with Jews in peril went without saying; and he helped wherever he could. Nor did he hesitate to visit the imprisoned Polish Metropolitan Dionysios. These activities were viewed with growing suspicion by the Nazi occupiers and Peradze's fruitful ecclesiastic and scientific activities were brought to an end in 1942 when, on May 4, he was arrested by the German Gestapo. [1] On December 6, 1942, Grigol Peradze was killed in the Nazi concentration camp of Auschwitz (O wi cim) when he entered a gas-chamber instead of a Jewish prisoner who had a large family.

Main fields of scientific activity of Grigol Peradze were: the history of the Georgian Orthodox and Apostolic Church, source studies of the history of Georgia and the Georgian Church, Patrology, history of Georgian literature, Rustvelology (Shota Rustaveli was a great Georgian poet of the 12th century), etc.

Grigol Peradze was canonized by the Georgian Orthodox and Apostolic Church in 1995. The Feast Day for St. Priest Martyr Grigol is December 6.

Some main scientific works of Grigol Peradze

- Die Anfänge des Mönchtums in Georgien.- "Zeitschrift für Kirchengeschichte", 47, Heft 1, Stuttgart, 1928, pp. 34-75 (in German)
- L'activité littéraire des moines géorgiens au monastère d'Iviron au mont Athos.- "Revue d'histoire ecclésiastique", 23, Fasc. 3, Paris, 1927, pp. 530-539 (in French)
- Über das georgische Mönchtum.- "Internationale Kirchliche Zeitschrift", 34, Heft 3, Bern, 1926, pp. 152-168 (in German)

o Die Probleme der ältesten Kirchengeschichte Georgiens.- "Oriens Christianus", 29, Bd. 7, Wiesbaden, 1932, pp. 153-171 (in German)
o Zur vorbyzantinischen Liturgie Georgiens.- "Le Museon", 42, Fasc. 2, Louvain, 1929, pp. 90-99 (in German)
o Les Monuments liturgiques prébyzantins en langue géorgienne.- "Le Museon", 45, Fasc. 4, Louvain, 1932, pp. 255-272 (in French)
o The Liturgy of Saint Peter.- "Kyrios", 2, Fasc. 3, 1937, pp. 260-262
o An Account of the Georgian Monks and Monasteries in Palestine as revealed in the Writings of Nongeorgian Pilgrims.- "Georgica", 2, Vol. 4-5, London, 1937, pp. 181-246
o Über die Georgischen Handschriften in Österreich.- "Wiener Zeitschrift für die Kunde des Morgenlandes", 47, Heft 3-4, Wien, 1940, pp. 219-232 (in German)
o Im Dienste der Georgischen Kultur.- "Aus der Welt des Ostens", Königsberg, 1940, pp. 30-50 (in German)

Notes and references (URLs online)

o 1. Lukas Vischer: A Georgian Saint: Grigol Peradze (1899-1942)

Literature about Grigol Peradze

o Victor Nozadze. "Grigol Peradze".- Georgian journal "Mamuli", Buenos-Aires, No 5, 1952
o Tamar Dularidze. About the life and death of Grigol Peradze.- "Russkaia Misl", New York, 13-19.VII, 1995 (In Russian)
o "Artanuji" (The Georgian historical scientific journal), Tbilisi, No 11, 2003 (Special issue: Grigol Peradze), 120 pp (In Georgian)
o David Kolbaia (editor) "St. Grigol (Peradze) works nr 1, in: Pro Georgia Journal of Kartvelological Studies nr 13, 200.

Websites (URLs online)

o Lukas Vischer: A Georgian Saint: Grigol Peradze (1899-1942)
o wiadkowie XX wieku - Grzegorz Peradze (in Polish)
o Sviaschennomuchenik Arkhimandrit Grigorii (Peradze) (in Russian)

A hyperlinked version of this chapter is at http://booksllc.net?q=Grigol%5FPeradze

8

ILIA CHAVCHAVADZE

Ilia Chavchavadze

- o Ilia Chavchavadze.
- o Born: November 8, 1837(1837-11-08) Kvareli, Kakheti, Georgia
- o Died: September 12, 1907 (aged 69) Tsitsamuri, outside Mtskheta, Georgia
- o Occupation: jurist, poet, novelist, humanist, publisher, philosopher
- o Nationality: Georgian
- o Period: 1863 - 1907
- o Literary movement: Realism and Historical fiction
- o Notable work(s): *Is a human a man?!*, *Letters of a Traveler*
- o Signature:

Prince **Ilia Chavchavadze** (Georgian:) (8 November [O.S. 27 October] 1837 12 September [O.S. 30 August] 1907) was a Georgian writer, poet, journalist and lawyer who spearheaded the revival of the Georgian national movement in the second half of the 19th century, during the Russian rule of Georgia. Today he is widely regarded as one of the founding fathers of modern Georgia. He was canonized as **Saint Ilia the**

Righteous ( ) by the Georgian Orthodox Church. Today, Georgians revere Ch avch avadze as *Pater Patriae* (Father of the Fatherland) of Georgia.[1]

Inspired by the contemporary liberal movements in Europe, as a writer and a public figure, Ilia Ch avch avadze directed much of his efforts toward awakening national ideals in Georgians and to the creation of a stable society in his homeland.

His most important literary works were: *The Hermit, The Ghost, Otaraant Widow, Kako The Robber* and *Is He Human, This "Man"?*. He was editor-in-chief of the Georgian periodicals *Sakartvelos Moambe* (1863 1877) and *Iveria* (1877 1905), and authored numerous articles for journals. Most of his work dealt with Georgia and Georgians. He was a devoted protector of the Georgian language and culture from Russification.

Chavchavadze was fatally wounded by a gang of assassins, led by Gigla Berbichashvili, in Tsitsamuri, outside Mtskheta. His legacy earned him the broad admiration of the Georgian people.

Life

Ancestry and early life

Ilia Ch avch avadze was born in Kvareli, a village located in the Alazani Valley, in the Kakheti province of Georgia, which was part of the Russian Empire at that time. Ilia was a *tavadi*, the Georgian title of duke. It is thought that the noble Ch avch avadze family came from the Pshav-Khevsureti region of Georgia, and, in 1726, King Constantine II granted the Ch avch avadze family the rank of Prince in recognition of their knighthood and valor to the nation. This resulted in the family moving and settling in the Alazani Gorge in Kakheti. According to King Erekle II's order, Ilia's great grandfather, Bespaz Ch avch avadze was knighted when he defeated twenty thousand Persian invaders in Kvareli in 1755.

Ilia was the third son of Grigol Ch avch avadze and Mariam Beburishvili. Grigol, like his father and his famous ancestors, had a military background. He, along with the local militiamen protected the village from numerous Dagestani invasions. This can be seen in the architecture of the Ilia Ch avch avadze museum house in Kvareli, incorporating a Medieval castle style in the two-storey castle in the yard, which was designed to protect the house during invasions.

Ilia's mother, Mariam, died on May 4, 1848, when Ilia was ten years old, and his father asked his sister, Makrine, to help bring up the children. *Aunt Makrine* had a significant impact on Ilia's life, because, after 1852, when Ilia's father Grigol died, she was the only remaining caretaker of the family.

Online image: Ilia Ch'avch'avadze in 1st Gymnasium of Tbilisi, 1848

Ch'avch'avadze was educated at the elementary level by the deacon of the village before he moved to Tbilisi where he attended the prestigious Academy for Nobility in 1848. However, from an early age, Ilia was influenced by his parents who were highly educated in classical literature, Georgian history and poetry. From his parents, Ilia learned the inspiring stories of Georgian heroism in classical historical novels. In his autobiography, Ilia refers to his mother, Princess Mariam Ch avch avadze, who knew most Georgian novels and poems by heart and encouraged her children to study them. Ilia also described the influence of the deacon's storytelling, which gave him an artistic inspiration, later applied in his novel writing.

In 1848, after the death of Princess Ch avch avadze, Ilia was sent to Tbilisi by his father to begin his secondary education. Ilia attended a private school for three years before he entered the 1st Academy of Tbilisi in 1851. Soon after, Ilia's father died and Aunt Makrine looked after the family. His secondary school years were very stressful, due to his father's death. However, the Ch avch avadze family suffered another devastating blow when Ilia s brother, Constantine, was killed during the Dagestani raid on Kakheti. Ilia expressed his anguish and grief in one of his first short-poems called *Sorrow of a Poor Man*. In addition to his personal problems, the political situation in Georgia worsened under the harsh authority of the Russian Empire, which played a destructive role to the nation and its culture.

Student years

Online image: Ilia Ch avch avadze during his studies at the university in Saint Petersburg, 1860

After graduating from the academy, Ilia decided to continue his education at the University of St. Petersburg, Russia. Before leaving for St. Petersburg, Ilia composed one of his most remarkable poems, *To the Mountains of Kvareli* in the village of Kardanakhi on April 15 of 1857, where he expressed his lifelong admiration for the Greater Caucasus Mountains and his sorrow at leaving his homeland.

That same year, Ilia was admitted to the University of St. Petersburg. During his student years, numerous revolutions sprang up in Europe which Ilia observed with great interest. Ilia's attention focused on the events in Italy and the struggle of Giuseppe Garibaldi, whom he admired for many years. While in St.Petersburg, Ilia met Princess Catherine Ch avch avadze, from whom he learned about the poetry and lyrics of the Georgian romantic Prince Nik'oloz Baratashvili. Due to the harsh climate in St Petersburg, Ilia became very ill and returned to Georgia for several months in 1859.

Ilia finally returned to Georgia after the completion of his studies in 1861. During his journey back, Ilia wrote one of his greatest masterpieces, *The Travelers' Diaries*, where he outlines the importance of nation-building and provides an allegorical comparison of Mt. Kazbegi and the Tergi River in the Khevi region of Georgia.

Political life

Online image: Newspaper "Iveria" (Iberia) founded and edited by Ch avch avadze during his political career. The newspaper focused on the national liberation movement of Georgia in the late 1800's.

Ilia s main political and social goals were based on Georgian patriotism. He radically advocated the revival of the use of the Georgian language, the cultivation of Georgian literature, the revival of autocephalous status for the Georgian national church, and, finally, the revival of Georgian statehood, which had ended when the country became part of the Russian Empire. As the number of supporters for his ideas grew, so did opposition among the leading Social Democrats and Bolsheviks like Noe Zhordania; their main aims were focused on battling the Tsarist autocracy and implementing Marxist ideology throughout the Russian empire. This did not include the revival of a Georgian state or of a Georgian self-identity. Ilia was viewed as bourgeois and as an old aristocrat who failed to realize the importance of the revolutionary tide.

In addition to his works described above, he was also the founder and chairman of many public, cultural and educational organizations (Society for the Spreading of Literacy Among Georgians, "The Bank of the Nobility", "The Dramatic Society", "The Historical-Ethnographical Society of Georgia", etc.). He was also a translator of British literature. His main literary works were translated and published in French, English, German, Polish, Ukrainian, Belarusian, Russian and other languages. Between 1906 and 1907, he was a member of the State Council (Gosudarstvennaya Duma) in Russia. His eclectic interests also led him to be a member of, among others, the Caucasian Committee of the Geographical Society of Russia, the Society of Ethnography and Anthropology of Moscow University, the Society of Orientalists of Russia and the Anglo-Russian Literary Society (London).

Prince Chavchavadze briefly acted as a literary mentor to a young Joseph Stalin, who was then an Orthodox seminarian in Tbilisi. According to historian Simon Sebag Montefiore,

"The Prince was sufficiently impressed to show the teenagers work to his editors. He admired Stalin's verse, choosing five poems to publish – quite an achievement. Prince Chavchavadze called Stalin the, 'young man with the burning eyes.'"[2]

Death

Online image: Prince Ch avch avadze's funeral in Tbilisi

After serving as a member of the Upper House in the first Russian Duma, Ilia decided to return to Georgia in 1907. On August 28, 1907 Ilia Ch avch avadze was murdered by a gang of six assassins who ambushed him and his wife Olga while traveling from Tbilisi to Saguramo, near Mtskheta. The assassination of Ilia Ch avch avadze remains controversial today. Based on recent discoveries in archives, the plot to assassinate Ilia is believed to have been a joint operation by the Mensheviks and the Bolsheviks, due to Ilia's condemnation of their violent terrorist ways, his socially conservative vision for Georgian nationalism, and his tremendous popularity among the public.

Author and historian Simon Sebag Montefiore suspects that a young Joseph Stalin may have been involved in planning the Prince's murder. According to Montefiore,

"The Bolshevik position in Georgia was undermined by the assassination of the hugely popular Prince Ilya Chavchavadze.. in August 1907. The Bolsheviks had attacked his patriarchal vision of Georgian culture and, it was widely believed, had decided to kill him; there is some evidence that Stalin's friend Sergo Ordzhonikidze organized or took part in the assassination. It may be that the SDs took no part in the murder at all. Stalin always praised Chavchavandze's poetry in his old age and there is no evidence that he ordered the hit, but he was very close to Sergo and he was certainly more than capable of separating literary merit from cruel necessity: politics always came first."[3]

During World War II, an old man confessed to having been hired by the Tsarist Okhrana to assassinate Ilia. During the Soviet period, an investigation was launched by the Soviet authorities which later concluded that the Tsarist secret police and administration had been involved in the assassination.

Either way, the Prince's murder was seen as a national tragedy which was mourned by all strata of Georgian society. Prince Ak'ak'i Tsereteli, who was suffering from serious health problems at the time, spoke at the funeral and dedicated an outstanding oration to Ilia: "Ilia's inestimable contribution to the revival of the Georgian nation is an example for future generations".[4]

Legacy

In 1987, Prince Chavchavadze was formally canonized by the Georgian Orthodox and Apostolic Church, as "Saint Ilia the Righteous."

Online image: Monument to Ch avch avadze (l) and Tsereteli (r) in front of the first Gymnasium in Tbilisi

As a result of Ilia's death, the Bolshevik terror grew, and the Georgian Social Democrats started to gain significant power and support among the population. Eventually, realizing their differences with the Bolsheviks, the Social Democrats of Georgia decided to revive Georgian statehood and proclaimed independence on May 26, 1918. After the Bolshevik occupation of Georgia and integration into the Soviet Union, Ilia became the national symbol of Georgian freedom and national liberation. In 1989, during the anti-Soviet protests in Tbilisi, the poems, novels and political life of Ilia Ch avch avadze became a driving force behind the Georgian struggle for independence.

The idea of National revival, which Ilia preached and advocated in various Georgian societies throughout his life, gained in momentum in 1990. In 2002, Mikheil Saakashvili, a young Georgian politician who was educated in the United States, created a movement which was to revive the old party of Ilia Ch avch avadze, known as the United National Movement. Mikheil Saakashvili s National Movement party played a major role in the peaceful Rose Revolution of 2003 which ousted President Eduard Shevardnadze.

Important publications of the works of Ilia Ch avch avadze

- *Georgische Dichter.* Translated and compilled by Arthur Leist, Dresden-Leipzig, 1887 (Poems of Ilia Ch avch avadze and other Georgian poets, in German)
- *The Hermit* by Prince Ilia Ch avch avadze. Translated from the Georgian by Marjory Wardrop, London, 1895

See also (online edition)

- List of Georgians
- History of Georgia
- Tbilisi Ilia Ch avch avadze State University Of Language and Culture

References (URLs online)

- 1. Socialism in Georgian Colors: The European Road to Social Democracy, 1883-1917, Stephen F. Jones
- 2. Simon Sebag Montefiore, "Young Stalin," page 57.
- 3. Simon Sebag Montefiore, "Young Stalin," page 179.
- 4. David Marshal Lang, History of Modern Georgia, p. 176.

Resources

- Baron de Baie: *Au nord de la chaine du Caucase souvenirs d'une mission"*, Paris, 1899 *(in French)*
- Baron de Baie: *Tiflis souvenirs d'une mission*, Paris, 1900 (in French)
- Companjen, Françoise J. , "Between Tradition and Modernity". Amsterdam 2004, pp. 167 171 (in English)
- Leist, Arthur: *Das georgische Volk*, Dresden, 1903 (in German)
- Lehman-Haupt, C.F. : *Reisen und Forschungen*, Berlin, 1910, pp. 106 111 (in German)
- Reisner, Oliver: *The Tergdaleulebi: Founders of Georgian National Identity*. In: Ladislaus Löb, István Petrovics, György E. Szonyi (eds.): *Forms of Identity: Definitions and Changes*. Attila Jozsef University, Szeged 1994, pp. 125 37
- Wardrop, Oliver *The Kingdom of Georgia*, London, 1888, pp. 150 152

Websites (URLs online)

A hyperlinked version of this chapter is at http://booksllc.net?q=Ilia%5FChavchavadze

9

KETEVAN GELADZE

Online image: Ekaterina Geladze (credited as Dzhugashvili) by Isaak Brodskiy.

Ketevan Geladze ("Ekaterina" in Russian, and familiarly known as "Keke") (February 5, 1858 June 4, 1937) was the mother of Joseph Stalin. She was born to a family of Georgian Orthodox Christian serfs in Gambareuli, Georgia, in 1858 and although her father, Glakh Geladze, died young and the family was always poor, somehow her mother Melania (née Homezurashvili) ensured that Keke learned to read and write.

Keke met and married Besarion Jughashvili at the age of 14. Her first two children died shortly after birth Mikhail in 1876 and Georgy the following year. Her third son (and last child), Joseph, was born on December 18, 1878 and survived. Nicknamed "Soso", Joseph grew up in a violent home: his father ("Beso") was incessantly drunk and beat his mother and him frequently. When Stalin's father beat Keke, Keke occasionally fought back. Before Joseph was 10, Beso left the family home (some sources say he was thrown out by his wife). To support herself and her son, Keke took on any menial job available mainly housework, sewing and laundering.

Keke often worked in the houses of rich Jewish traders in Gori, and sometimes took her son along. He was said to have been a smart child and he entertained some of the householders, including David Pismamedov who encouraged the young Stalin to study, and gave him money and books to read.

His mother's ambition was for Joseph to become a priest and she somehow accumulated enough money for his education, perhaps with Pismamedov's help. In 1888 she was able to enroll Soso into the Gori Church School and, later, with his mother's encouragement, he obtained a scholarship to the Tiflis Theological Seminary, a Georgian Orthodox institution which he attended from the age of sixteen.

Later in life, when Stalin achieved prominence in the communist regime, he installed his mother in a palace in the Caucasus, formerly used by the tsar's viceroy. There she is said to have occupied only one tiny room from where she wrote frequent letters (in Georgian she never managed to learn good Russian) to her son and daughter-in-law.

These were reciprocated, although Stalin is believed not to have visited her until 1935, when she was very sick. N. Kipshidze, a doctor who treated Keke in her old age, recalled that Stalin asked his mother at this meeting: "Why did you beat me so hard?" "That's why you turned out so well", Keke answered. In return, his mother asked him: "Joseph–who exactly are you now?" "Remember the tsar? Well, I'm like a tsar", replied Stalin. "You'd have done better to have become a priest" was his mother's retort. She died on May 13, 1937.[1]

References (URLs online)

- 1. Edvard Radzinsky, p. 32

- Simon Sebag Montefiore, "Young Stalin," 2007.
- Edvard Radzinsky: Stalin: The First In-depth Biography Based on Explosive New Documents from Russia's Secret Archives, Anchor, (1997) ISBN 0-385-47954-9

A hyperlinked version of this chapter is at http://booksllc.net?q=Ketevan%5FGeladze

10

KETEVAN OF KAKHETI

Online image: St. Queen Ketevan of Kakheti (a Georgian Orthodox fresco)

Ketevan, "the Martyr" (Georgian: , *ketevan ts'amebuli*) (1565 September 13, 1624) was a queen of Kakheti, a kingdom in eastern Georgia. She was killed at Shiraz, Iran, after prolonged tortures for refusing to give up the Christian faith and embrace Islam.

Ketevan was born to Prince Ashotan of Mukhrani (Bagrationi) and married Prince David of Kakheti, the future David I, king of Kakheti from 1601 to 1602. After David s death, Ketevan engaged in religious building and charity. However, when David s brother Constantine I killed his reigning father, Alexander II, and usurped the crown with the Safavid Iranian support in 1605, Ketevan rallied the Kakhetian nobles against the patricide and routed Constantine s loyal force. After the uprising, she negotiated with Shah Abbas I of Iran to confirm her underage son, Teimuraz I, as king of Kakheti, while she assumed the function of a regent.

In 1614, sent by Teimuraz as a negotiator to Abbas I, Ketevan effectively surrendered herself as an honorary hostage in a failed attempt to prevent Kakheti from being attacked by the Iranian armies. She was held in Shiraz for several years until Abbas I, in an act of revenge for the recalcitrance of Teimuraz, ordered the queen to renounce Christianity, and upon her refusal, had her tortured to death with red-hot pincers in 1624. Portions of her relics were clandestinely taken by the St. Augustine Portuguese Catholic missioners, eyewitnesses of her martyrdom, to Georgia where they were interred at the Alaverdi Cathedral.[1] The rest of her remains are reported to have been buried at the St. Augustine Church in Goa, India. Several expeditions from Georgia have arrived in Goa, and searched in vain for the exact location of her grave.[2][3]

Queen Ketevan was canonized by Zachary, Catholicos-Patriarch of Georgia (1613-1630) and September 26 was instituted by the Georgian Orthodox Church as the day of her commemoration.

The account of Ketevan's martyrdom related by the Augustinians missioners were exploited by her son, Teimuraz, in his poem *The Book and Passion of Queen Ketevan* (, *ts'igni da ts'ameba ketevan dedoplisa*; 1625) as well as by the German author Andreas Gryphius in his classical tragedy *Katharine von Georgien* (1657).[4] The Georgian monk Grigol Dodorkeli-Vakhvakhishvili of the David Gareja Monastery was another near-contemporaneous author whose writings, a hagiographic work as well as several hymns, focuse on Ketevan's life and martyrdom.

The Augustinian Friars exhumed her body after four months and took the relics to Georgia and interred them at the Alaverdi Cathedral, and also brought a hand and palm to Goa.

After the Archeological Survey of India started excavations to conserve the site at St Augustine's complex two decades back, in 2004-05, archaeologists found three bones in the chapter chapel in the convent of St Augustine.

Scientists have conducted a DNA analysis on bones believed to have been relics of Georgian queen Ketevan preserved in St Augustine's complex at Old Goa, but the mystery continues as a matching analysis of her other relics in Georgia needs to be done to confirm the findings.

References (URLs online)

o 1. Suny, Ronald Grigor (1994), *The Making of the Georgian Nation: 2nd edition*, pp. 50-51. Indiana University Press, ISBN 0253209153.
o 2. Georgians seek buried bones of martyred queen. *The Guardian*. June 25, 2000. Cited by *The Iranian*. Accessed on October 26, 2007.
o 3. Georgia - Basic facts. Ministry of External Affairs, Government of India. February, 2007. Accessed on October 26, 2007.
o 4. Rayfield, Donald (2000), *The Literature of Georgia: A History*, pp. 105-106. Routledge, ISBN 0-7007-1163-5.

o Lang, David Marshall (1976). *Lives and Legends of the Georgian Saints*. New York: Crestwood. (Excerpt "The Passion of Queen Ketevan")

A hyperlinked version of this chapter is at http://booksllc.net?q=Ketevan%5Fof% 5FKakheti

11

LASHA ZHVANIA

Lasha Zhvania

- Minister for Economic Development of Georgia
- **Incumbent**
- **Assumed office** 9 December 2008
- President: Mikheil Saakashvili
- Prime Minister: Zurab Noghaideli
- Chairman of the Parliamentary Foreign Affairs Committee
- **In office** 14 June 2008 9 December 2008
- President: Mikheil Saakashvili
- Preceded by: Konstantin Gabashvili
- Succeeded by: Zurab Pololikashvili
- Ambassador of Georgia in Israel
- **In office** 18 March 2005 7 June 2008
- President: Mikheil Saakashvili
- Prime Minister: Lado Gurgenidze
- Deputy Minister of Foreign Affairs
- **In office** 2004 2005
- President: Mikheil Saakashvili

○ Born: 14 October 1973 Tbilisi, Georgia
○ Spouse(s): Tea Kiknavelidze
○ Religion: Orthodox Christian

Lasha Zhvania (Georgian:) (born October 14, 1973 in Tbilisi, Georgia) is a Georgian politician, the Minister for Economic Development from November 2008 till August 2009 and an ex-Parliament of Georgia. A lawyer by education specializing in international law, he has served in the posts of Consul in Israel, Deputy-Minister of Finance, Deputy-Minister of Foreign Affairs, and Ambassador Extraordinary and Plenipotentiary to the State of Israel and the Republic of Cyprus, Chairman of the Foreign Relations Committee of the Parliament of Georgia.

Early life and career

Lasha Zhvania was born and raised in Tbilisi, Georgian SSR. He was educated at Tbilisi school No 1 (1979-1990), Faculty of International Law and International Relations of the Tbilisi State University (1990-1995), PHD study on International Humanitarian and Refugee Law at the Department for International Law of the Tbilisi State University (1995-1998). Apart from numerous high-profile government positions Zhvania has been actively involved in various educational Programmes attending the **CPDS** - Courses for Political and Diplomatic Studies in UK's Leeds University, in 1995, and Refugee and IDP International Law Programme at Birmingham University in UK, in 1998.

In addition to his native Georgian, he speaks English, Hebrew, Russian and Greek. Zhvania was elected to the Parliament on May 21, 2008. His appointment as Chairman for Foreign Relations Committee on 14 June 2008 coincided with Georgia s increasingly tense relations with its northern neighbor Russia over the breakaway regions of Abkhazia and South Ossetia, and Georgia s aspiration to join NATO.

He is married to Tea Kiknavelidze and they have three children - Anna, Sulkhan-Irineos and Helen.[1][2]

References (URLs online)

○ 1. Parliament web site
○ 2. Invest in Georgia news

A hyperlinked version of this chapter is at http://booksllc.net?q=Lasha%5FZhvania

12

LUARSAB II OF KARTLI

Online image: Luarsab II, a 19th-century artistic notion by Mikhail Sabinin

The Holy Martyr **Luarsab II** (Georgian: II) (1592 21 June (O.S.), 4 July (N.S.), 1622), of the Bagrationi dynasty, was a king of Kartli (eastern Georgia) from 1606 to 1615. He is known for his martyr s death at the hands of the Persian shah Abbas I. The Georgian Orthodox Church regards him as saint and marks his memory on the day of his death, July 4.

Luarsab ascended the Kartlian throne at the age of 14 after his father, Giorgi X, suddenly died in 1606. During his minority, the government was actually run by a royal tutor Shadiman Baratashvili. It was when Abbas I succeeded in driving the Ottoman armies out of eastern Georgia, leaving a Persian force in Tbilisi, and confirming Luarsab as king of Kartli. The Ottomans attempted to remove Luarsab, sending in Georgia a large army, only to be destroyed by the Georgian general Giorgi Saakadze at the Battle of Tashiskari, 1609. After this victory, Luarsab was granted again the control of the citadel of Tbilisi and the shah married his sister Tinatin, 1610. Late in 1611, Luarsab himself married Makrine, a sister of a lower-class noble

Saakadze. The great nobles of the realm led by Shadiman Baratashvili convinced the king that Saakadze was a Persian agent seeking a royal crown. They induced Luarsab to divorce Makrine and forced Saakadze into exile to Persia. Shah Abbas indeed demanded more loyalty and obedience from the Georgians and encouraged a khan of Kazan Mohamed to trouble the Kartlian lands. In 1612, Luarsab had Mohamed assassinated and allied with another Georgian monarch, Teimuraz I of Kakheti to counter an anticipated Persian aggression. Early in 1614, a large Persian army invaded Kakheti, destroying several settlements on its way, and moved into Kartli. Luarsab and Teimuraz fled to a western Georgian Kingdom of Imereti. George III of Imereti refused to surrender the refugees. Abbas threatened Kartli with ruin, promising that if Luarsab submitted, he would conclude a peace. In October 1615, Luarsab surrendered to save his kingdom from being wiped out, and, refusing to covert to Islam, was incarcerated first in the fortress of Astarabad, and then in Shiraz. The Georgians attempted to free their king through the mediation of a Tsar Mikhail I of Russia. However, the negotiations yielded no results and, in 1622, Luarsab was executed (strangled with a bow string) on the orders of the shah.

Websites (URLs online)

- (Georgian) Luarsab I
- (Georgian) Luarsab the Martyr, an essay by Ilia Chavchavadze, 1886.
- (English) The Orthodox Church in America website
- (English) Kings of Kartli at *Royal Ark* website

Preceded by **George X**: **King of Kartli** 1606 1615: Succeeded by **Bagrat VII**

A hyperlinked version of this chapter is at http://booksllc.net?q=Luarsab%5FII%5Fof%5FKartli

13

PATRIARCH CALLISTRATUS OF GEORGIA

Callistratus (Georgian: , *Kalistrate*) (April 24, 1866 February 2, 1952) was a Catholicos-Patriarch of All Georgia from June 21, 1932 until his death. His full title was *His Holiness and Beatitude, Archbishop of Mtskheta-Tbilisi and Catholicos-Patriarch of All Georgia.*

Educated at the theological seminaries of Tiflis and Kiev, he was ordained to the priesthood at the Didube Church in 1893. He then served at the Kashueti Church (1903) and was involved in the Georgian autocephalist movement in defense of which he produced, in 1905, a special study of the Georgian Orthodox Church, which had been under the Russian control since 1810. After the reestablishment of the Georgian church in 1917, he was consecrated metropolitan at Ninotsminda in 1925 and bishop at Manglisi in 1927. After the imprisonment of Catholicos Patriarch Ambrose by the Soviet government, Callistratus was a *locum tenens* from 1923 to 1926. After his election to the patriarchate in 1932, following a brief reign of Christophorus III, Callistratus tried to pursue a conciliatory line with the Stalin's regime in order to ease the pressure from authorities. Through Stalin's mediation, Callistratus reconciled the Georgian church with its Russian counterpart, which in turn recognized the Georgian autocephaly in 1943. In 1948, he was appointed to the Soviet Peace Committee. Despite official Soviet atheist propaganda, Callistratus maintained that Christianity and Communism could coexist.[1][2] He died in 1952 and was interred at the Tbilisi Sioni Cathedral.

References (URLs online)

o 1. Shirley, Eugene B. (1991), *Candle in the wind: religion in the Soviet Union*, p. 42. Ethics and Public Policy Center
o 2. Kolarz, Walter (1962), *Religion in the Soviet Union*, p. 103. Macmillan

Preceded by **Christophorus III**: **Catholicos-Patriarch of All Georgia** 1932 1952: Succeeded by **Melchizedek III**

A hyperlinked version of this chapter is at http://booksllc.net?q=Patriarch%5FCallistratus%5Fof%5FGeorgia

14

PATRIARCH CHRISTOPHORUS III OF GEORGIA

Christophorus III (Georgian: III, *K'ristep'ore III*) (March 27, 1873 January 10, 1932) was a Catholicos-Patriarch of All Georgia from 1927 until his death.

He was born as **Kristepore Tsitskishvili** ( ) near the town of Kharagauli. Having graduated from the Tiflis Theological Seminary in 1895, he served as a priest in the Trans-Caspian region, and later in Georgia. At the same time, he taught theology and Georgian, and was energetically involved in the movement which led to the restoration of autocephaly of the Georgian Orthodox Church in 1917. Christophorus was consecrated as a bishop of Urbnisi (1921-1925) and metropolitan of Abkhazia (1925-1927). Elected as the catholicos-patriarch on June 4, 1927, he had to lead the Georgian church under harsh pressure from the Soviet authorities.

References (URLs online)

o (Georgian) Catholicoi and Patriarchs of Georgia. *Orthodoxy.Ge*

Preceded by **Ambrose**: **Catholicos-Patriarch of All Georgia** 1927 1932: Succeeded by **Callistratus**

A hyperlinked version of this chapter is at http://booksllc.net?q=Patriarch%5FChristophorus%5FIII%5Fof%5FGeorgia˙

15

PATRIARCH DAVID V OF GEORGIA

David V (Georgian: V, born as **Khariton Devdariani** ( ) (April 6, 1903 November 9, 1977) was a Catholicos-Patriarch of All Georgia from July 2, 1972, until his death. His full title was *His Holiness and Beatitude, Archbishop of Mtskheta-Tbilisi and Catholicos-Patriarch of All Georgia.*

Born in the village of Mirotsminda (now Kharagauli municipality, Imereti), David became a priest in 1927 and a bishop in 1956. From 1959 to 1972 he served as a chorbishop to Catholicos-Patriarch Ephraim II, upon whose death he succeeded as the prelate of the Georgian Orthodox Church.

David V s ascension to the patriarchal sea was followed by some controversy. Unlike his predecessor Ephraim II, who frequently appealed to the Georgian patriotism, David never gained popularity because of his perceived loyalty to the Soviet regime. Furthermore, Georgian dissidents suspected the Soviet security (KGB) was involved in David s election by rigging it and destroying Ephraim's will which had allegedly endorsed Bishop Ilia of Sukhumi and Abkhazia as his successor. Georgian nationalist underground claimed in their *samizdat* publications corruption and moral depravity flourished in the church under David V who was also accused of being involved, along with the Georgian Communist party officials and the Russian KGB, in robbery of the Georgian church treasures.[1]

David V died in Tbilisi and was buried at the Sioni Cathedral in 1977. He was succeeded by Ilia II, whom the Soviets had allegedly tried to keep out of office.[1]

Reference

- o 1. Ramet, Sabrina P. (1989), Religion and Nationalism in Soviet and East European Politics, pp. 35-6. Duke University Press, ISBN 0822308916

Preceded by **Ephraim II**: **Catholicos-Patriarch of All Georgia** 1972 1977: Succeeded by **Ilia II**

A hyperlinked version of this chapter is at http://booksllc.net?q=Patriarch%5FDavid%5FV%5Fof%5FGeorgia

16

PATRIARCH EPHRAIM II OF GEORGIA

Ephraim II (Georgian: II, *Eprem*) (October 19, 1896 April 7, 1972) was a Catholicos-Patriarch of All Georgia from 1960 until his death. His full title was *His Holiness and Beatitude, Archbishop of Mtskheta-Tbilisi and Catholicos-Patriarch of All Georgia.*

Born as Grigol Sidamonidze ( ), the future prelate graduated from the Tiflis Theological Seminary in 1918 and from the Tbilisi State University with a degree in philosophy in 1925. He became a monk in 1922. At various times, from 1927 to 1960, he served as bishop of Nikortsminda, bishop of Gelati and Kutaisi, and metropolitan of Batumi-Shemokmedi and Chkondidi. After the death of Melchizedek III in 1960, Ephraim was elected to the office of Catholicos-Patriarch of Georgia. During his tenure, Ephraim tried to avoid confrontation with the Soviet government, but produced a series of sermons, appealing to the Georgian patriotism, for which he gained popularity.[1] At the same time, he cultivated friendly ties with the Russian Orthodox Church and the Armenian Apostolic Church and, in 1962, brought the Georgian church into the World Council of Churches (of which it would remain a member until 1997).[2] He died in 1972 and was interred at the Tbilisi Sioni Cathedral.

References (URLs online)

○ 1. (Russian) , (1983), . In: . Accessed on October 25, 2009.
○ 2. Max Hayward, William C. Fletcher (1969), *Religion and the Soviet State: a Dilemma of Power*, p. 179. Praeger

Preceded by **Melchizedek III**: **Catholicos-Patriarch of All Georgia** 1960 1972: Succeeded by **David V**

A hyperlinked version of this chapter is at http://booksllc.net?q=Patriarch%5FEphraim%5FII%5Fof%5FGeorgia

17

PATRIARCH ILIA II OF GEORGIA

Ilia II

- *Catholicos-Patriarch of Georgia*
- Church: Georgian Orthodox Church
- Enthroned: December 25, 1977
- Reign ended: Incumbent
- Predecessor: David V
- Personal details
- Birth name: Irakli Ghudushauri-Shiolashvili (-)
- Born: 4 January 1933 (1933-01-04) Vladikavkaz, Russia
- Denomination: Greek Orthodox Christianity
- Occupation: Catholicos-Patriarch
- Profession: Theologian
- Alma mater: Moscow clerical seminary
- Signature:

Ilia II (also transliterated as Ilya or Elijah; Georgian: II) (born January 4, 1933) is the current Catholicos-Patriarch of All Georgia and the spiritual leader of the Georgian

Orthodox Church. He is officially styled as *His Holiness and Beatitude, Archbishop of Mtskheta-Tbilisi and Catholicos-Patriarch of All Georgia.*

Biography

Ilia II was born as **Irakli Ghudushauri-Shiolashvili** (-) in Vladikavkaz, Russia's North Ossetia. He is a descendant of the influential eastern Georgian mountainous clan with family ties with the former royal dynasty of the Bagrationi.

He graduated from the Moscow clerical seminary and was ordained a hierodeacon in 1957 and hieromonk in 1959; he graduated from the Moscow clerical academy in 1960 and returned to Georgia, where he was assigned to the Batumi Cathedral Church as a priest. In 1961, he was promoted to hegumen and later to archimandrite. On August 26, 1963, he was chosen to be the bishop of Batumi and Shemokmedi and appointed a patriarchal vicar. From 1963 to 1972 he was also the first rector of the Mtskheta Theological Seminary - the only clerical school in Georgia at that time.

In 1967, he was consecrated as the bishop of Tskhumi and Abkhazeti and elevated to the rank of metropolitan in 1969. After the death of the controversial Patriarch David V, he was elected the new Catholico-Patriarch of Georgia on December 25, 1977. He began a course of reforms, enabling the Georgian Orthodox Church, once suppressed by the Soviet ideology, largely regain its former influence and prestige by the late 1980s. In 1988 there were 180 priests, 40 monks, and 15 nuns for the faithful, who were variously estimated as being from one to three million. There were 200 churches, one seminary, three convents, and four monasteries. During the last years of the Soviet Union, he was actively involved in Georgia's social life. He joined the people demonstrating in Tbilisi against the Soviet rule on April 9, 1989, and fruitlessly urged the protesters to withdraw to the nearby Kashueti Church to avoid the bloodshed. This peaceful demonstration was dispersed by the Soviet troops, leaving behind 22 dead and hundreds injured. During the civil war in Georgia in the 1990s, he called the rival parties to find a peaceful solution to the crisis.

From 1978 to 1983, Ilia II was Co-President of the World Council of Churches (WCC), an ecumenical organization the Georgian Orthodox Church had joined with other Soviet churches in 1962. In May 1997, the Holy Synod of the Georgian Orthodox Church announced its withdrawal from the WCC.

As patriarch, he has received the highest Church awards from the Patriarchs of the Orthodox Churches of Antioch, Jerusalem, Alexandria, Russia, Greece, Bulgaria, Romania and almost all other Orthodox Churches.

As a productive theologian and church historian, he was conferred an Honorary Doctorate of Theology from St. Vladimir's Orthodox Theological Seminary in New York (1986), the Academy of Sciences in Crete (1997) and the St. Tikhon's Orthodox Theological Seminary in Pennsylvania (1998).

Ilia II is an Honorary Academician of: the Georgian Academy of Sciences (2003) and the International Academy for the Promotion of Scientific Research (2007). In February 2008, his grace was awarded the David Guramishvili Prize

Ilia II is known as a proponent of a constitutional monarchy as a form of government for Georgia. On October 7, 2007, Ilia II he publicly called, in his sermon, to consider establishing a constitutional monarchy under the Bagrationi dynasty which had been dispossessed by the Russian Empire of the Georgian crown early in the 19th century.[1] The statement coincided with the rising confrontation between the government of President Mikheil Saakashvili and the opposition many members of which welcomed the patriarch's proposal.[2]

During the August 2008 Russian-Georgian war, Ilia II appealed to the Russian political leadership and the church, expressing concerns that "the Orthodox Russians were bombing Orthodox Georgians," and dismissing the Russian accusations of Georgia s "genocide" in South Ossetia as "pure lie". He also made a pastoral visit, bringing food and aid, to the Russian-occupied central Georgian city of Gori and the surrounding villages which were at the verge of humanitarian catastrophe. He also helped retrieve bodies of deceased Georgian soldiers and civilians.[3][4] Ilia II also blessed the September 1, 2008 "Stop Russia" demonstrations in which tens of thousands organized human chains across Georgia.[5]

In December 2008, Ilia II visited Moscow to pay a final farewell to Russia s late Patriarch Alexy II. On December 9, 2008, he met Russia s President Dmitry Medvedev, which was the first high-level official contact between the two countries since the August war.[6] Later, Ilia II announced that he had some "positive agreements" with Medvedev which needed "careful and diplomatic" follow-up by the politicians.[7]

Ilia II has spurred a baby boom in the nation by opting to personally baptize any third child born after his initiative started. The result was a national baby boom because being baptized by the head patriarch is a huge honor in Georgia.[8]

References (URLs online)

- o 1. Georgian Church Calls for Constitutional Monarchy. Civil Georgia. 2007-10-07.
- o 2. Politicians Comment on Constitutional Monarchy Proposal. Civil Georgia. 2007-10-10.
- o 3. War splits Orthodox churches in Russia and Georgia. the International Herald Tribune. September 5, 2008
- o 4. Church Intervenes to Bring Soldiers Bodies Back. Civil Georgia. 2008-08-16
- o 5. Georgians in Mass Live Chain Say Stop Russia . Civil Georgia. 2008-09-01
- o 6. Head of Georgian Church Meets Medvedev. Civil Georgia. 2008-09-01
- o 7. Head of Georgian Church Again Speaks of Positive Agreements with Medvedev. Civil Georgia. 2008-12-16
- o 8. http://news.bbc.co.uk/2/hi/europe/7964302.stm

Websites (URLs online)

- ○ Catholicos-Patriarch of all Georgia(In Georgian language)

A hyperlinked version of this chapter is at http://booksllc.net?q=Patriarch%5FIlia%5FII%5Fof%5FGeorgia

18

PATRIARCH KYRION II OF GEORGIA

Online image: Kyrion II, Catholicos-Patriarch of All Georgia. 1917

Kyrion II (Georgian: II) (November 10, 1855 26 June 1918) was a Georgian religious figure and historian who served as the first Catholicos-Patriarch of All Georgia after the restoration of independence (autocephaly) of the Georgian Orthodox Church from the Russian Orthodox Church in 1917 until his assassination in 1918. He was canonized by the Georgian Holy Synod in 2002.

Life

Kyrion II was born as Giorgi Sadzaglishvili ( ) in the village of Nikozi, Georgia (then part of the Tiflis Governorate, Imperial Russia), into the family of a priest. He graduated from the seminaries of Tbilisi (1876) and Kiev (Kyiv) (1880), and was appointed a deputy inspector of the Odessa Seminary in 1880. Returning to Georgia in 1883, he served both as a teacher at the theological schools in Gori, Kutaisi and Tbilisi, and a church official. At the same time, under the pseudonyms of Iverieli and Nikozeli, he published several works, in Georgian and Russian, about the history of the Georgian Orthodox Church and Christianity in Georgia. He discovered and studied several unique medieval Georgian manuscripts, collected old Georgian coins, recorded pieces of folklore, sponsored talented Georgian students, and collaborated with foreign scholars interested in Georgia.

After the death of his wife and children, he became a monk, assumed the name of Kyrion, and was ordained to the position of archimandrite at Kvatakhevi Monastery in 1896. He served as a bishop at Alaverdi (1898-1901) and Gori (1901-2). In the early 1900s, during the heated debates concerning the status of the Georgian church, he was an active proponent of the Georgian autocephalist movement, calling for the restoration of the autocephalous Orthodox Church of Georgia abolished by Imperial Russia in 1811. For this reason, he was removed from Georgia to Kamenets-Podolsk (now Kamianets-Podilskyi, Ukraine) (1902) and later to Kovno (now Kaunas, Lithuania) (1903). In 1908, the Russian Exarch of Georgia, Archbishop Nikon, was murdered in Tbilisi, and the Russian government exploited the situation as a pretext for removing Georgian bishops from their posts.[1] Kyrion was deprived of the title of bishop, sent to Kuriazh, Ukraine, and later confined into Sanaksar Monastery, Russia. In 1915, he was restored to his rank and appointed a bishop of Polotsk and Vitebsk. He was able to return to Georgia only after the 1917 February Revolution in St Petersburg led to a de facto secession of Georgia from Russia. Returning to Georgia in September 1917, he was welcomed by Georgians as their spiritual leader. By that time, Georgian clergymen had restored the autocephaly of the Georgian church (March 12, 1917), and Kyrion was elected as Catholicos Patriarch and consecrated at Svetitskhoveli Cathedral on October 1, 1917. The Most Holy Synod of the Russian Orthodox Church refused to recognize the move, and the result was a break in communion between the two churches.[2] At the same time, he faced an opposition from a group of Georgian priests who defied his authority. Kyrion s death remains a mystery to this day. He was found at his residence at Martqopi Monastery in the morning of June 27 1918 murdered. He was buried at Tbilisi Sioni Cathedral. The Holy Synod of the Georgian Orthodox Church canonized him on October 17, 2002.[3][4]

References (URLs online)

o 1. Lang, David M. (1962), *A Modern History of Georgia*, p. 178. London: Weidenfeld and Nicolson.
o 2. It was not until 1943 that the Russian Orthodox Church recognized the autocephaly of the Georgian Patriarchate and the relations between the two co-religionist churches were restored.
o 3. (Georgian) - II - - (*The Life of Saints The Priest Martyr Kyrion II Catholicos Patriarch of All Georgia*). Accessed on April 6, 2007.
o 4. (Georgian) II ("Kyrion II"), an article by Sergo Vardosanidze. Accessed on April 6, 2007.

Preceded by **Russian Exarchate of Georgia**: **Catholicos-Patriarch of All Georgia** 1917 1918: Succeeded by **Leonid**

A hyperlinked version of this chapter is at http://booksllc.net?q=Patriarch%
5FKyrion%5FII%5Fof%5FGeorgia

19

PATRIARCH LEONID OF GEORGIA

Leonid (Leonidas) (Georgian: , **Leonide**) (1860 1921) was a Catholicos-Patriarch of All Georgia from 1918 to 1921.

Born Longinoz Okropiridze ( ) in Georgia, then part of Imperial Russia, he graduated from the Theological Academy of Kiev in 1888. He was later involved in missionary activities, chiefly in the Caucasus. He served as an inspector of the schools operated by the Society for the Restoration of Orthodox Christianity in the Caucasus, an organization established by the Russian authorities. From the 1890s to the 1910s, he served as an archimandrite of the monasteries of Zedazeni, Khirsi, and of St. John the Baptist in Georgia. He also chaired the Commission for Correction of the Georgian Bible, and was a member to the Georgia-Imeretia Synodal office. Leonid was actively involved in the Georgian autocephalist movement which succeeded in restoration of the independent Georgian church from the Russian Orthodox Church in 1917. During 1918, he functioned as a bishop of Gori, Imereti, Guria-Samegrelo, and as a metropolitan of Tbilisi. On November 28, 1918, following the murder of Kyrion II, he was elected a Catholicos-Patriarch of All Georgia. During his tenure, he faced several problems such as the lack of international recognition of the Georgian autocephaly, and the persecution of the Georgian church by the Bolshevik regime established by the invading Russian army in February 1921. Leonid died on June 11, 1921, during the cholera epidemics in the Georgian SSR.

References (URLs online)

(Georgian) " ". In: *Encyclopaedia Georgiana* (Georgian Soviet Encyclopedia). Vol. 6. 1982.

Preceded by **Kyrion II**: **Catholicos-Patriarch of All Georgia** 1918 1921: Succeeded by **Ambrose**

A hyperlinked version of this chapter is at http://booksllc.net?q=Patriarch%5FLeonid%5Fof%5FGeorgia

20

PATRIARCH MELCHIZEDEK III OF GEORGIA

Melchizedek III (Georgian: III) (1872 January 10, 1960) was a Catholicos-Patriarch of All Georgia from 1952 until his death. His full title was *His Holiness and Beatitude, Archbishop of Mtskheta-Tbilisi and Catholicos-Patriarch of All Georgia.*

Born as Mikheil Pkhaladze ( ) in the Tiflis Governorate, Russian Empire, the future prelate received his education at the theological colleges of Tiflis and Kazan. He then taught at various seminaries in Russia and Georgia. In 1915, Melchizedek was ordained to priesthood. When the Georgian Orthodox Church broke free of Russian control in 1917, he returned to homeland and, in 1922, became a priest at the Tbilisi Sioni Cathedral and then at Anchiskhati. He then served as a bishop at Alaverdi (1925-27), archbishop at Sukhumi (1927-28), chief priest at the Tbilisi Church of Transfiguration (1928-1935), metropolitan of Sukhumi and Abkhazia (1935-38), and chief priest at the Tbilisi Didube Church (1944-52). After the death of Callistratus, Melchizedek was elected as Catholicos-Patriarch of All Georgia in 1952. Despite pressure from the Soviet government, he was able to reopen the churches of Bodbe, Motsameta and Ilori during his tenure.[1]

References (URLs online)

- 1. Wieczynski, Joseph L. (ed., 1976), *The Modern Encyclopedia of Russian and Soviet History*, Vol. 21, p. 189. Academic International Press, ISBN 0875690645

Preceded by **Callistratus**: **Catholicos-Patriarch of All Georgia** 1952 1960: Succeeded by **Ephraim II**

A hyperlinked version of this chapter is at http://booksllc.net?q=Patriarch%5FMelchizedek%5FIII%5Fof%5FGeorgia

21

TORNIKIOS

T'ornike (Georgian:) also known as **Tornikios** or **Thornikios** (Greek: , died in 985) was a retired Georgian general and monk who came to be better known as a founder of the formerly Georgian Orthodox Iviron Monastery on Mt Athos in the modern-day northeastern Greece.

Tornike came from a notable Georgian noble family and was in the immediate circles of the ruling dynasty of the Bagrationi. His father, Chordvaneli, had been in the suite of the Georgian prince Ashot II Kuropalates who had paid a visit to the Byzantine emperor Constantine Porphyrogennetos in Constantinople in c. 950. Three of his nephews had military careers and one of them, Varazvache, held a post of *katepano* (military governor) of the significant Byzantine eastern outpost Edessa in 1037-8.

T'ornike served a very successful military and courtier career (specifically he was *eristavi*, a Georgian equivalent to *strategos*) under the Georgian Bagratid dynasty and also gained the Byzantine title of *patrikios*. He resigned his position as a general of the Georgian prince David III of Tao in c. 963 and, under the name of Ioane (Ioannis, or John), retired to Athanasius Lavra on Mount Athos. He was joined, in the early 970s, by another retired Georgian officer Ioane and his son Ek'vt'ime.

In 976, a rebellion led by Bardas Skleros broke out in the Asian provinces of the Byzantine Empire, a greatest upheaval of the emperor Basil II s early reign. Skleros had won a series of battles against the then-loyal general Bardas Phokas and marched from the east through Anatolia to Constantinople. Basil summoned Ioane-T ornike to his capital to mediate the alliance with David III of Tao, a measure that seemed to be necessary to save the situation. The monk agreed reluctantly, persuaded chiefly by his fellow monks that it would be in the best interests of the Athonite community for him to obey the imperial command. David responded vigorously and entrusted his former general the command of some 12,000 Georgian cavalrymen sent to reinforce the imperial army. The decisive battle was fought at Pankalia near Caesarea on March 24, 979 and resulted in the crushing defeat of the rebels.

In reward for their support, David was awarded with the lifetime stewardship of the extensive lands in northeastern Anatolia, while Ioane-T'ornike was conferred with the title *synkellos* (assistant to patriarch). More importantly, the victorious monk-general returned to Athos laden with the spoils of war, "precious objects" as well as twelve kentenaria (1,200 lb) of gold, that enabled the Georgians to establish their own house on Athos, called Iviron. Although populated now with Greeks, the monastery is to this day known by the Greek appellation *Iveron*, "of the Iberians", i.e., Georgians. The emperor also showered him with lands and privileges, granted him subsidies and exemption from taxes. The new monastic house, destined to become a vibrant center of the Georgian Orthodox culture, was jointly run by Ioane-T ornike as *ktetor* (founder) and his friend Ioane as *hegoumenos* (abbot).

References (URLs online)

o Morris, R. (2002), *Monks and Laymen in Byzantium*, 843-1118, Cambridge University Press (UK), ISBN 0-521-26558-4, pp 85-6
o Peelers P. Un Colophon georgien de Thornik le moine // Analecta Bollandiana, 1932-50

Websites (URLs online)

o Greek Monasteries, URL accessed on June 16, 2006

A hyperlinked version of this chapter is at http://booksllc.net?q=Tornikios

22

ZVIAD GAMSAKHURDIA

Zviad Gamsakhurdia

- o 1st President of Georgia
- o **In office** April 14, 1991 January 6, 1992
- o Preceded by: *Nobody*
- o Succeeded by: Eduard Shevardnadze
- o Born: March 31, 1939(1939-03-31) Tbilisi, Georgian SSR, Soviet Union
- o Died: December 31, 1993 (aged 54) Khibula, Georgia
- o Nationality: Georgian

Zviad Gamsakhurdia[1] (Georgian: , (March 31, 1939 December 31, 1993) was a dissident, scientist and writer, who became the first democratically elected President of the Republic of Georgia in the post-Soviet era. Gamsakhurdia is the only Georgian President to have died whilst formally in office.

Gamsakhurdia as dissident

Early career

Zviad Gamsakhurdia was born in the Georgian capital Tbilisi in 1939, in a distinguished Georgian family; his father, Academician Konstantine Gamsakhurdia (1893 1975), was one of the most famous Georgian writers of the 20th century. Perhaps influenced by his father, Zviad received training in philology and began a professional career as a translator and literary critic.

Despite (or perhaps because of) the country's association with Stalin, Soviet rule in Georgia was particularly harsh during the 1950s and sought to restrict Georgian cultural expression. In 1955, Zviad Gamsakhurdia established a youth underground group which he called the *Gorgasliani* (a reference to the ancient line of Georgian kings) which sought to circulate reports of human rights abuses. In 1956, he was arrested during demonstrations in Tbilisi against the Soviet policy of russification and was arrested again in 1958 for distributing anti-communist literature and proclamations. He was confined for six months to a mental hospital in Tbilisi where he was diagnosed as suffering from "psychopathy with decompensation", thus perhaps becoming an early victim of what became a widespread policy of using psychiatry for political purposes.

Human rights activism

He achieved wider prominence in 1972 during a campaign against the corruption associated with the appointment of a new Catholicos of the Georgian Orthodox Church, of which he was a "fervent"[2] adherent. He co-founded the Initiative Group for the Defense of Human Rights in 1973, became the first Georgian member of Amnesty International in 1974 and co-founded the Georgian Helsinki Group in 1976 (renamed the Georgian Helsinki Union in 1989). Gamsakhurdia was Chairman of this human rights organization. He was very active in the underground network of *samizdat* publishers, contributing to a wide variety of underground political periodicals including *Okros Satsmisi* ("The Golden Fleece"), *Sakartvelos Moambe* ("The Georgian Herald"), *Sakartvelo* ("Georgia"), *Matiane* ("Annals") and *Vestnik Gruzii*. He participated in the Moscow underground periodical "Chronicle of Current Events", edited by Sergey Kovalev. Gamsakhurdia was also the first Georgian member of the International Society for Human Rights (ISHR-IGFM).

Perhaps seeking to emulate his father, Zviad Gamsakhurdia also pursued a distinguished academic career. He was a Senior Research Fellow of the Institute of Georgian Literature of the Georgian Academy of Sciences (1973 1977, 1985 1990), Associate Professor of the Tbilisi State University (1973 1975, 1985 1990) and member of the Union of Georgia's Writers (1966 1977, 1985 1991), PhD in the field of Philology (1973) and Doctor of Sciences (Full Doctor, 1991). He wrote a number of important literary works, monographs and translations of British, French and American literature, including translations of works by T. S. Eliot, William Shakespeare, Charles Baudelaire and Oscar Wilde. He was also an outstanding Rustvelologist (Shota Rustaveli was a great Georgian poet of the 12th century) and researcher of history of the Iberian-Caucasian culture.

Although he was frequently harassed and occasionally arrested for his dissidence, for a long time Gamsakhurdia avoided serious punishment, probably as a result of his family's prestige and political connections. His luck ran out in 1977 when the activities of the Helsinki groups in the Soviet Union became a serious embarrassment to the Soviet government of Leonid Brezhnev. A nationwide crackdown on human rights activists was instigated across the Soviet Union. In Georgia, the government of Eduard Shevardnadze (who was then First Secretary of the Georgian Communist Party) arrested Gamsakhurdia and his fellow dissident Merab Kostava. The two men were sentenced to three years' hard labour plus three years' exile for "anti-Soviet activities". Their imprisonment attracted international attention[3], leading to members of the United States Congress nominating Gamsakhurdia and Kostava for the Nobel Peace Prize in 1978 (though it went to Anwar Sadat and Menachem Begin instead). Kostava was exiled to Siberia, while Gamsakhurdia was exiled to the Russian autonomous republic of Dagestan.

At the end of June 1979, Gamsakhurdia was released from jail and pardoned in controversial circumstances after serving only two years of his sentence (Kostava remained in prison until 1987). The authorities claimed that he had confessed to the charges and recanted his beliefs; a film clip was shown on Soviet television to substantiate their claim.[4] According to a transcript published by the Soviet news agency TASS, Gamsakhurdia spoke of "how wrong was the road I had taken when I disseminated literature hostile to the Soviet state. Bourgeois propaganda seized upon my mistakes and created a hullabaloo around me, which causes me pangs of remorse. I have realized the essence of the pharasaic campaign launched in the West, camouflaged under the slogan of 'upholding human rights.'"

His supporters, family and Merab Kostava claimed that his recantation was coerced by the KGB, and although he publicly acknowledged that certain aspects of his anti-Soviet endeavors were mistaken, he did not renounce his leadership of the dissident movement in Georgia. Perhaps more importantly, his actions ensured that the dissident leadership could remain active. Kostava and Gamsakhurdia later both independently stated that the latter's recantation had been a tactical move. In an open letter to Shevardnadze, dated April 19, 1992, Gamsakhurdia claimed that "my so-called confession was necessitated ... [because] if there was no 'confession' and my release from the prison in 1979 would not have taken place, then there would not have been a rise of the national movement."[5]

Gamsakhurdia returned to dissident activities soon after his release, continuing to contribute to *samizdat* periodicals and campaigning for the release of Merab Kostava. In 1981 he became the spokesman of the students and others who protested in Tbilisi about the threats to Georgian identity and the Georgian cultural heritage. He handed a set of "Demands of the Georgian People" to Shevardnadze outside the Congress of the Georgian Writers Union at the end of March 1981, which earned him another spell in jail.

Moves towards independence

Online image: Leaders of Georgian independence movement in late 80s, Zviad Gamsakhurdia (left) and Merab Kostava (right)

When the Soviet leader Mikhail Gorbachev initiated his policy of glasnost, Gamsakhurdia played a key role in organizing mass pro-independence rallies held in Georgia between 1987 1990, in which he was joined by Merab Kostava on the latter's release in 1987. In 1988, Gamsakurdia became one of the founders of the Society of Saint Ilia the Righteous (SSIR), a combination of a religious society and a political party which became the basis for his own political movement. The following year, the brutal suppression by Soviet forces of a large peaceful demonstration held in Tbilisi in April 4 9, 1989 proved to be a pivotal event in discrediting the continuation of Soviet rule over the country. The progress of democratic reforms was accelerated and led to Georgia's first democratic multiparty elections, held on October 28, 1990. Gamsakhurdia's SSIR party and the Georgian Helsinki Union joined with other opposition groups to head a reformist coalition called "Round Table Free Georgia" ("Mrgvali Magida Tavisupali Sakartvelo"). The coalition won a convincing victory, with 64% of the vote, as compared with the Georgian Communist Party's 29.6%. On November 14, 1990, Zviad Gamsakhurdia was elected by an overwhelming majority as Chairman of the Supreme Council of the Republic of Georgia.

Georgia held a referendum on restoring its pre-Soviet independence on March 31, 1991 in which 90.08% of those who voted declared in its favour. The Georgian parliament passed a declaration of independence on April 9, 1991, in effect restoring the 1918-21 Georgian state. However, it was not recognized by the Soviet Union and although a number of foreign powers granted early recognition, universal recognition did not come until the following year. Gamsakhurdia was elected President in the election of May 26 with 86.5% per cent of the vote on a turnout of over 83%.

Gamsakhurdia as President

On taking office, Gamsakhurdia was faced with major economic and political difficulties, especially regarding Georgia's relations with the Soviet Union. A key problem was the position of Georgia's many ethnic minorities (making up 30% of the population). Although minority groups had participated actively in Georgia's return to democracy, they were underrepresented in the results of the October 1990 elections with only nine of 245 deputies being non-Georgians. Even before Georgia's independence, the position of national minorities was contentious and led to outbreaks of serious inter-ethnic violence in Abkhazia during 1989.

In 1989, violent unrest broke out in South Ossetian Autonomous Oblast between the Georgian independence-minded population of the region and Ossetians loyal to the Kremlin. South Ossetia's regional soviet announced that the region would secede from Georgia to form a "Soviet Democratic Republic". In response, the Georgian Supreme Soviet annulled the autonomy of South Ossetia in March 1990.[6]

A three-way power struggle between Georgian, Ossetian and Soviet military forces broke out in the region, which resulted (by March 1991) in the deaths of 51 people and the eviction from their homes of 25,000 more. After his election as Chairman of the newly renamed Supreme Council, Gamsakhurdia denounced the Ossetian move as being part of a Russian ploy to undermine Georgia, declaring the Ossetian separatists to be "direct agents of the Kremlin, its tools and terrorists." In February 1991, he sent a letter to Mikhail Gorbachev demanding the withdrawal of Soviet army units and an additional contingent of interior troops of the USSR from the territory of former Authonomous District of South Ossetia.

According to George Khutsishvili, the nationalist "Georgia for the Georgians" hysteria launched by the followers of Gamsakhurdia "played a decisive role" in "bringing about Bosnia-like inter-ethnic violence."[7]

Human Rights violations criticism

On December 27, 1991, U.S. based Helsinki Watch NGO issued a report on Human Rights violations made by the government of Gamsakhurdia.[8] The report included information on documented Freedom of Assembly, Freedom of Speech, Freedom of the Press violations in Georgia, on Political Imprisonment, Human Rights abuses by Georgian government and paramilitary in South Ossetia, and other human Rights violations.

The rise of the opposition

Gamsakhurdia's opponents were highly critical of what they regarded as "unacceptably dictatorial behaviour", which had already been the subject of criticism even before his election as President. Prime Minister Tengiz Sigua and two other senior ministers resigned on August 19 in protest against Gamsakhurdia's policies. The three ministers joined the opposition, accusing him of "being a demagogue and totalitarian" and complaining about the slow pace of economic reform. In an emotional television broadcast, Gamsakhurdia claimed that his enemies were engaging in "sabotage and betrayal" within the country.

Gamsakhurdia's response to the coup against President Gorbachev was a source of further controversy. On August 19, Gamsakhurdia, the Georgian government, and the Presidium of the Supreme Council issued an appeal to the Georgian population to remain calm, stay at their workplaces, and perform their jobs without yielding to provocations or taking unauthorized actions. The following day, Gamsakhurdia appealed to international leaders to recognize the republics (including Georgia) that had declared themselves independent of the Soviet Union and to recognise all legal authorities, including the Soviet authorities deposed by the coup. He claimed publicly on August 21 that Gorbachev himself had masterminded the coup in an attempt to boost his popularity before the Soviet presidential elections, an allegation rejected as "ridiculous" by US President George H. W. Bush.

In a particularly controversial development, the Russian news agency Interfax reported that Gamsakhurdia had agreed with the Soviet military that the Georgian National Guard would be disarmed and on August 23 he issued decrees abolishing the post of commander of the Georgian National Guard and redesignating its members as interior troops subordinate to the Georgian Ministry of Internal Affairs. In reality, the National Guard was already a part of the Ministry of the Interior, and Gamsakhurdia's opponents, who claimed he was seeking to abolish it, were asked to produce documents they claimed they possessed which verified their claims, but did not do so. Gamsakhurdia always maintained he had no intention of disbanding the National Guard (source: Zviad Gamsakhurdia, The Nomenklatura Revanche in Georgia, Soviet Analyst, 1993). In defiance of the alleged order of Gamskhurdia, the sacked National Guard commander Tengiz Kitovani led most of his troops out of Tbilisi on August 24. By this time, however, the coup had clearly failed and Gamsakhurdia publicly congratulated Russia's President Boris Yeltsin on his victory over the putschists (Russian Journal "Russki Curier", Paris, September, 1991). Georgia had survived the coup without any violence, but Gamsakhurdia's opponents accused him of not being resolute in opposing it.

Gamsakhurdia reacted angrily, accusing shadowy forces in Moscow of conspiring with his internal enemies against Georgia's independence movement. In a rally in early September, he told his supporters: "The infernal machinery of the Kremlin will not prevent us from becoming free... Having defeated the traitors, Georgia will achieve its ultimate freedom." He shut down an opposition newspaper, "Molodiozh Gruzii," on the grounds that it had published open calls for a national rebellion. Giorgi Chanturia, whose National Democratic Party was one of the most active opposition groups at that time, was arrested and imprisoned on charges of seeking help from Moscow to overthrow the legal government. It was also reported that Channel 2, a television station, was closed down after employees took part in rallies against the government.[9]

The government's activities aroused controversy at home and strong criticism abroad. A visiting delegation of US Congressmen led by Representative Steny Hoyer reported that there were "severe human rights problems within the present new government, which is not willing to address them or admit them or do anything about them yet." American commentators cited the human rights issue as being one of the main reasons for Georgia's inability to secure widespread international recognition. The country had already been granted recognition by a limited number of countries (including Romania, Turkey, Canada, Finland, Ukraine, the Baltic States and others) but recognition by major countries eventually came during Christmas 1991, when the U.S., Sweden, Switzerland, France, Belgium, Pakistan, India and others formally recognized Georgian independence.

The political dispute turned violent on September 2, when an anti-government demonstration in Tbilisi was dispersed by police. The most ominous development was the splintering of the Georgian National Guard into pro- and anti-government factions, with the latter setting up an armed camp outside the capital. Skirmishes between the two sides occurred across Tbilisi during October and November with occasional fatalities resulting from gunfights. Paramilitary groups one of the largest of which was the anti-Gamsakhurdia "Mkhedrioni" ("Horsemen" or "Knights"), a nationalist militia with several thousand members set up barricades around the city.

Coup d'état

On December 22, 1991, armed opposition supporters launched a violent coup d'etat and attacked a number of official buildings including the Georgian parliament building, where Gamsakhurdia himself was sheltering. Heavy fighting continued in Tbilisi until January 6, 1992, leaving at least 113 people dead. On January 6, Gamsakhurdia and members of his government escaped through opposition lines and made their way to Azerbaijan where they were denied asylum. Armenia finally hosted Gamsakhurdia for a short period and rejected Georgian demand to extradite Gamsakhurdia back to Georgia. In order not to complicate tense relations with Georgia, Armenian authorities allowed Gamsakhurdia to move to the breakaway Russian republic of Chechnya, where he was granted asylum by the rebellious government of General Dzhokhar Dudayev.

It was later claimed (although apparently not confirmed) that Soviet forces had been involved in the coup against Gamsakhurdia. On December 15, 1992 the Russian newspaper *Moskovskie Novosti* ("Moscow News") printed a letter claiming that the former Vice-Commander of the Trans-Caucasian Military District, Colonel General Sufian Bepaev, had sent a "subdivision" to assist the armed opposition. If the intervention had not taken place, it was claimed, "Gamsakhurdia's supporters' victory would be guaranteed." It was also claimed that Soviet special forces had helped the opposition to attack the state television tower on December 28.

A Military Council made up of Gamsakhurdia opponents took over the government on an interim basis. One of its first actions was to formally depose Gamsakhurdia as President. It reconstituted itself as a State Council and appointed Gamsakhurdia's old rival Eduard Shevardnadze as chairman in March 1992. The change in power was effected as a *fait accompli*, without any formal referendum or elections. He ruled as *de facto* president until the formal restoration of the presidency in November 1995.

Gamsakhurdia in exile

After his overthrow, Gamsakhurdia continued to promote himself as the legitimate president of Georgia. He was still recognized as such by some governments and international organizations, although as a matter of pragmatic politics the insurrectionist Military Council was quickly accepted as the governing authority in the country. Gamsakhurdia himself refused to accept his ouster, not least because he had been elected to the post with an overwhelming majority of the popular vote (in conspicuous contrast to the undemocratically appointed Shevardnadze). In November-December 1992, he was invited to Finland (by the Georgia Friendship Group of the Parliament of Finland) and Austria (by the International Society for Human Rights). In both countries, he held press conferences and meetings with parliamentarians and government officials (source: Georgian newspaper *Iberia-Spektri*, Tbilisi, December 15 21, 1992).

Clashes between pro- and anti-Gamsakhurdia forces continued throughout 1992 and 1993 with Gamsakhurdia supporters taking captive government officials and government forces retaliating with reprisal raids. One of the most serious incidents occurred in Tbilisi on June 24, 1992, when armed Gamsakhurdia supporters seized the state television center. They managed to broadcast a radio message declaring that "The legitimate government has been reinstated. The red junta is nearing its end." However, they were driven out within a few hours by the National Guard. They may have intended to prompt a mass uprising against the Shevardnadze government, but this did not materialize.

Shevardnadze's government imposed a harshly repressive regime throughout Georgia to suppress "Zviadism", with security forces and the pro-government Mkhedrioni militia carrying out widespread arrests and harassment of Gamsakhurdia supporters. Although Georgia's poor human rights record was strongly criticized by the international community, Shevardnadze's personal prestige appears to have convinced them to swallow their doubts and grant the country formal recognition. Government troops moved into Abkhazia in September 1992 in an effort to root out Gamsakhurdia's supporters among the Georgian population of the region, but well-publicized human rights abuses succeeded only in worsening already poor ethnic relations. Later, in September 1993, a full-scale war broke out between Georgian forces and Abkhazian separatists. This ended in a decisive defeat for the government, with government forces and 300,000 Georgians being driven out of Abkhazia and an estimated 10,000 people being killed in the fighting.

The 1993 civil war

Gamsakhurdia soon took up the apparent opportunity to bring down Shevardnadze. He returned to Georgia on September 24, 1993, establishing what amounted to a "government in exile" in the western Georgian city of Zugdidi. He announced that he would continue "the peaceful struggle against an illegal military junta" and concentrated on building an anti-Shevardnadze coalition drawing on the support of the regions of Samegrelo (Mingrelia) and Abkhazia. He also built up a substantial military force that was able to operate relatively freely in the face of the weak state security forces. After initially demanding immediate elections, Gamsakhurdia took advantage of the Georgian army's rout to seize large quantities of weapons abandoned by the retreating government forces. A civil war engulfed western Georgia in October 1993 as Gamsakhurdia's forces succeeded in capturing several key towns and transport hubs. Government forces fell back in disarray, leaving few obstacles between Gamsakhurdia's forces and Tbilisi. However, Gamsakhurdia's capture of the economically vital Georgian Black Sea port of Poti threatened the interests of Russia, Armenia (totally landlocked and dependent on Georgia's ports) and Azerbaijan. In an apparent and very controversial *quid pro quo*, all three countries expressed their support for Shevardnadze's government, which in turn agreed to join the Commonwealth of Independent States. While the support from Armenia and Azerbaijan was purely political, Russia quickly mobilized troops to aid the Georgian government. On October 20, around 2,000 Russian troops moved to protect Georgian railroads and provided logistical support and weapons to the poorly armed government forces. The uprising quickly collapsed and Zugdidi fell on November 6.

Gamsakhurdia's death

On December 31, 1993, Zviad Gamsakhurdia died in circumstances that are still unclear. It is known that he died in the village of Khibula in the Samegrelo region of western Georgia and later was re-buried in the village Jikhashkari (in the Samegrelo region also). According to British press reports, the body was found with a single bullet wound to the head. A variety of reasons have been given for his death, which is still controversial and remains unresolved:

Suicide

Gamsakhurdia's widow later told the Interfax news agency that her husband shot himself on December 31 when he and a group of colleagues found the building where he was sheltering surrounded by forces of the pro-Shevardnadze Mkhedrioni militia. The Russian media reported that his bodyguards heard a muffled shot in the next room and found that Gamsakhurdia had killed himself with a shot to the head from a Stechkin pistol. The Chechen authorities published what they claimed was Gamsakhurdia's suicide note: "Being in clear conscience, I commit this act in token of protest against the ruling regime in Georgia and because I am deprived of the possibility, acting as the president, to normalize the situation, to restore law and order". Most observers outside Georgia accept the view that his death was self-inflicted.

Died in infighting

Online image: gravestone of President Gamsakhurdia in Tbilisi

The Georgian Interior Ministry under Shevardnadze's regime suggested that he had either been deliberately killed by his own supporters, or had died following a quarrel with his former chief commander, Loti Kobalia.

Gamsakhurdia's death was announced by the Georgian government on January 5, 1994. Some refused to believe that Gamsakhurdia had died at all but this question was eventually settled when his body was recovered on February 15, 1994. Zviad Gamsakhurdia's remains were re-buried in the Chechen capital Grozny on February

24, 1994. On March 3, 2007, the newly appointed pro-Russian president of Chechnya Ramzan Kadyrov announced that Gamsakhurdia's grave - lost in the debris and chaos of a war-ravaged Grozny - was found in the center of the city. The remains of Gamsakhurdia were identified by Russian experts in Rostov-on-Don, and arrived in Georgia on March 28, 2007, for reburial. He was interred alongside other prominent Georgians at the Mtatsminda Pantheon on April 1, 2007.[10] Thousands of people throughout Georgia had arrived in Mtskheta's medieval cathedral to pay tribute to Gamsakhurdia.[11] "We are implementing the decision which was [taken] in 2004 to bury President Gamsakhurdia on his native soil. This is a fair and absolutely correct decision," President Mikheil Saakashvili told reporters, the *Civil Georgia* internet news website reported on 31 March.

He and his second wife Manana had two sons.

Legacy

On January 26, 2004, in a ceremony held at the Kashueti Church of Saint George in Tbilisi, the newly elected President Mikhail Saakashvili officially rehabilitated Gamsakhurdia to resolve the lingering political effects of his overthrow in an effort to "put an end to disunity in our society", as Saakashvili put it. He praised Gamsakhurdia's role as a "great statesman and patriot" and promulgated a decree granting permission for Gamsakhurdia's body to be reburied in the Georgian capital, declaring that the "abandon[ment of] the Georgian president's grave in a war zone ... is a shame and disrespectful of one's own self and disrespectful of one's own nation". He also renamed a major road in Tbilisi after Gamsakhurdia and released 32 Gamsakhurdia supporters imprisoned by Shevardnadze's government in 1993-1994, who were regarded by many Georgians and some international human rights organizations as being political prisoners.

Gamsakhurdia's supporters continue to promote his ideas through a number of public societies. In 1996, a public, cultural and educational non-governmental organization called the Zviad Gamsakhurdia Society in the Netherlands was founded in the Dutch city of 's-Hertogenbosch. It now has members in a number of European countries.

On September 3, 2008 his son Tsotne Gamsakhurdia was arrested on Tbilisi airport for alleged espionage for Russia. He is currently accused of espionage, conspiracy against the Government and inflicting bodily harm on a person [12]

Selected works

- *20th century American Poetry* (a monograph). Ganatleba, Tbilisi, 1972 (Georgian)
- *The Man in the Panther's Skin" in English*, a monograph, Metsniereba, Tbilisi, 1984, 222 pp. (In Georgian, English summary).
- "Goethe's Weltanschauung from the Anthroposophic point of view.", *Tsiskari*, Tbilisi, No 5, 1985 (Georgian)

o *Tropology (Image Language) of "The Man in the Panther's Skin"*, monograph). Metsniereba, Tbilisi, 1991 (Georgian)
o *Collected articles and Essays*. Khelovneba, Tbilisi, 1991 (Georgian)
o *The Spiritual mission of Georgia* (1990)
o *The Spiritual Ideals of the Gelati Academy* (1989)
o "Dilemma for Humanity", *Nezavisimaia Gazeta*, Moscow, May 21, 1992 (Russian)
o "Between deserts" (about the creative works of L. N. Tolstoy), *Literaturnaia Gazeta*, Moscow, No 15, 1993 (Russian)
o *Fables and Tales*. Nakaduli, Tbilisi, 1987 (Georgian)
o *The Betrothal of the Moon* (Poems). Merani, Tbilisi, 1989 (Georgian)

References (URLs online)

o 1. Particularly in Soviet-era sources, his patronymic is sometimes given as *Konstantinovich* in the Russian style.
o 2. Kolstø, Pål. *Political Construction Sites: Nation-Building in Russia and the Post-Soviet States*, p. 70. Westview Press, Boulder, Colorado, 2000.
o 3. U.S. vs. U.S.S.R.: Two on a Seesaw, *TIME Magazine*, July 10, 1978
o 4. GEORGIA 1992: Elections and Human Rights at British Helsinki Human Rights Group website
o 5. Zviad Gamsakhurdia, Open Letter to Eduard Shevardnadze at a Geocities Georgian-dedicated website
o 6. Hastening The End of the Empire, *TIME Magazine*, January 28, 1991
o 7. Intervention in Transcaucasus, George Khutsishvili, *Perspective*, Volume IV, No 3 (February-March 1994) Boston University
o 8. Human Rights Violations by the Government of Zviad Gamsakhurdia (Helsinki Watch via Human Rights Watch), December 27, 1991
o 9. Nicholas Johnson: Georgia Media 1990s at University of Iowa website
o 10. *Reburial for Georgia ex-president*. The BBC News. Retrieved on April 1, 2007.
o 11. Thousands Pay Tribute to the First President, *Civil Georgia*, March 31, 2007
o 12. (Russian)

Links and literature

o President Zviad Gamsakhurdia's Memorial Page
o Reports of the International Society for Human Rights (ISHR-IGFM)
o Reports of the British Helsinki Human Rights Group (BHHRG)
o Georgian Media in the 90s: a Step To Liberty
o Country Studies: Georgia U.S. Library of Congress
o SHAVLEGO
o [1] "The Lion in Winter My Friend Zviad Gamsakhurdia", Todor Todorev, May 2002
o Zviad Gamsakhurdia. "Open Letter to E. Shevardnadze"
o Zviad Gamsakhurdia. "The Nomenklatura Revanche in Georgia"
o "The Transcaucasian Republics and the Coup", Elizabeth Fuller, August 1991

Media articles and references (URLs online)

o "Soviets Release Penitent Dissident" *The Washington Post*, June 30, 1979 o "New Leaders Show Their Old Habits; Georgia, Some Other Soviet Republics Cling to Authoritarian Ways" *The Washington Post*, September 18, 1991

o (Russian) "Russki Curier", Paris, September, 1991.

o (Finnish) Aila Niinimaa-Keppo. "Shevardnadzen valhe" ("The Lie of Shevardnadze"), Helsinki, 1992.

o (German) Johann-Michael Ginther, "About the Putch in Georgia" *Zeitgeschehen - Der Pressespiegel* (Sammatz, Germany), No 14, 1992.

o "Repression Follows Putsch in Georgia!" "Human Rights Worldwide", Frankfurt/M., No 2 (Vol. 2), 1992.

o (Finnish) "Purges, tortures, arson, murders..." *Iltalehti* (Finland), April 2, 1992.

o (Finnish) "Entinen Neuvostoliito". Edited by Antero Leitzinger. Publishing House "Painosampo", Helsinki, 1992, pp. 114-115. ISBN 952-9752-00-8.

o "Attempted Coup Blitzed in Georgia; Two Killed" *Chicago Sun-Times*, June 25, 1992.

o "Moskovskie Novosti" ("The Moscow News"), December 15, 1992.

o (Georgian) "Iberia-Spektri", Tbilisi, December 15 21, 1992.

o J. "Soviet Analyst". Vol. 21, No: 9-10, London, 1993, pp. 15-31.

o Otto von Habsburg.- *ABC* (Spain). November 24, 1993.

o Robert W. Lee. "Dubious Reforms in Former USSR".- *The New American*, Vol. 9, No 2, 1993.

o (English)/(Georgian) "Gushagi" (Journal of Georgian political émigrés), Paris, No 1/31, 1994. ISSN 0763-7247, OCLC 54453360.

o Mark Almond. "The West Underwrites Russian Imperialism" *The Wall Street Journal*, European Edition, February 7, 1994.

o "Schwer verletzte Menschenrechte in Georgien" *Neue Zürcher Zeitung*. August 19, 1994.

o "Intrigue Marks Alleged Death Of Georgia's Deposed Leader" *The Wall Street Journal*. January 6, 1994

o "Georgians dispute reports of rebel leader's suicide" *The Guardian* (UK). January 6, 1994

o "Ousted Georgia Leader a Suicide, His Wife Says" *Los Angeles Times*. January 6, 1994

o "Eyewitness: Gamsakhurdia's body tells of bitter end" *The Guardian* (UK). February 18, 1994.

o (German) Konstantin Gamsachurdia: "Swiad Gamsachurdia: Dissident Präsident Märtyrer", Perseus-Verlag, Basel, 1995, 150 pp. ISBN 3-907564-19-7.

o Robert W. Lee. "The "Former" Soviet Bloc." *The New American*, Vol. 11, No 19, 1995.

o "CAUCASUS and unholy alliance." Edited by Antero Leitzinger. ISBN 952-9752-16-4. Publishing House "Kirja-Leitzinger" (Leitzinger Books), Vantaa (Finland), 1997, 348 pp.

o (Dutch) "GEORGIE 1997" (Report of the Netherlands Helsinki Union/NHU), s-Hertogenbosch (The Netherlands), 1997, 64 pp.

o "Insider Report" *The New American*, Vol. 13, No 4, 1997.

o Levan Urushadze. "The role of Russia in the Ethnic Conflicts in the Caucasus."- CAUCASUS: War and Peace. Edited by Mehmet Tutuncu, Haarlem (The Netherlands), 1998, 224 pp. ISBN 90-901112-5-5.

o "Insider Report" *The New American*, Vol. 15, No 20, 1999.

o "Gushagi", Paris, No 2/32, 1999. OCLC 54453360.

o (Dutch) Bas van der Plas. "GEORGIE: Traditie en tragedie in de Kaukasus." Publishing House "Papieren Tijger", Nijmegen (The Netherlands), 2000, 114 pp. ISBN 90-6728-114-X.

o (English) Levan Urushadze. "About the history of Russian policy in the Caucasus."-
   IACERHRG's Yearbook 2000, Tbilisi, 2001, pp. 64-73.

Preceded by **Soviet era**: **President of Georgia** 1991 1992: Succeeded by **Eduard
Shevardnadze**

A hyperlinked version of this chapter is at http://booksllc.net?q=Zviad%
5FGamsakhurdia

INDEX

's-Hertogenbosch, 74
[du rd v rdn dz], 12

Abbas I, 41
Abbas I of Iran, 35
Abkhazeti, 52
Abkhazia, 14, 40, 45, 61, 72
Academy of Sciences, 52
Adrianopol, 1
Ajaria, 14, 16
Alaverdi, 56, 61
Alaverdi Cathedral, 36
Alazani, 28
Aleksandr Bessmertnykh, 11, 18
Alexander II, 35
Alexandria, 52
Alexy II, 53
Alma mater, 51
Ambrose, 43, 46, 60
Amnesty International, 66
Anatolia, 64
Anchiskhati, 61
Andreas Gryphius, 36
Andrei Gromyko, 11, 13
Andrey Gromyko, 18
Andrey Kozyrev, 11, 18

Andronikashvili, 9
anti-Soviet protests, 31
Antim Cup, 2
Antim Monastery, 2
Antioch, 52
Anwar Sadat, 67
Arabic, 2
Arabic fonts, 2
Archimandrite, 23
archimandrite, 52, 56, 59
Armenia, 73
Armenian, 6
Armenian Apostolic Church, 49
Arthur Leist, 32
Ashot II Kuropalates, 63
Asian, 64
Aslan Abashidze, 16
assassinated, 2
assassination, 55
Astarabad, 42
Athanasius, 64
atheist, 44
Auditing Commission, 12
Auschwitz, 24
Austria, 24
autocephalist, 43, 59

Eastern Orthodox Christians From Georgia (Country).

autocephaly, 45, 55
Azerbaijan, 15, 73

Baden-Baden, 16
Bagrat VII, 42
Bagrationi, 35, 41, 52, 63
Baltic States, 70
Bardas Phokas, 64
Bardas Skleros, 64
Basil II, 64
Battle of Tashiskari, 41
Batumi, 49, 52
BBC, 18
BBC News, 75
Belarusian, 30
Besarion Jughashvili, 33
Bible, 59
Birmingham University, 40
bishop, 43, 45, 47, 52, 56, 59
bishop of Nikortsminda, 49
black-market, 12
Bodbe, 61
Bolshevik, 60
Bolshevik Russia, 20
Bolsheviks, 9, 31
Bolshevism, 12
Boris Pankin, 11, 18
Boris Yeltsin, 70
Boston University, 75
British, 30
British Helsinki Human Rights Group, 75
Bucharest, 1
Bulgaria, 2, 24, 52
Byzantine, 63
Byzantine title, 63

Caesarea, 64
Callistratus, 46, 61, 62
Canonized, 1
canonized, 2, 27, 31
capitalism, 12
castle, 28
Catholic, 36
Catholicos, 66
Catholicos-Patriarch of All Georgia, 43–51, 55,
          56, 59–62
Catholicos-Patriarch of Georgia, 36
Caucasian Iberia, 2
Caucasus, 20, 34, 59
cavalrymen, 64
Central Committee, 12, 13
Ch avch avadze, 28
Charles Baudelaire, 66
Charles de Gaulle, 20
Chechen, 14

Chechen Republic, 14
Chechnya, 14, 71
cholera, 60
chorbishop, 47
Christian, 35
Christianity, 56
Christophorus III, 43, 44
chronic pneumonia, 6
Chronicle of Current Events, 66
Church Slavonic, 2
Civil Georgia, 53
civil war in Georgia, 52
classical literature, 29
classical philosophy, 2
cobbler, 5, 6
Colin Powell, 16
colitis, 6
collapse of the Soviet Union, 14
Commonwealth of Independent States, 73
Communism, 44
Communism portal, 13
Communist Party, 67
Communist Party of the Soviet Union, 12
concentration camp, 24
Congress, 12
consecrated, 52
Constantin Brâncoveanu, 2
Constantine I, 35
Constantine II, 28
Constantine Porphyrogennetos, 63
Constantinople, 63
Constituent Assembly, 20
constitutional monarchy, 53
Control Committee, 12
corruption, 15
coup d'etat, 71
CPSU, 11
Crete, 52
culture, 20
Czechoslovakia, 16

détente, 13
Dagestan, 67
Dagestani, 28, 29
David Gareja Monastery, 36
David Guramishvili Prize, 53
David I, 35
David III of Tao, 63, 64
David V, 50, 52
de facto, 56
deacon, 29
Democratic Republic of Georgia, 20
democratically, 65
dissident, 65
Dmitry Medvedev, 53

drinking problem, 6
drunken, 6
duke, 28
Dzhokhar Dudayev, 71

Eastern Orthodox, 1
ecclesiastic, 23
ecumenical, 52
Ecumenical Patriarchate of Constantinople, 2
Edessa, 63
Eduard Shevardnadze, 32, 65, 67, 71, 77
Ek'vt'ime, 64
Ekaterina (Keke) Geladze, 6
elected, 65
Encyclopædia Britannica, *Eleventh Edition*, 2
end of the Cold War, 13
English, 30
Ephraim II, 47, 48, 62
epidemics, 60
Erekle II, 28
ethnic Georgian, 2
Europe, 28, 29
European, 20
European Union, 15
events in Italy, 29
exiled, 2

Feast, 1
February Revolution, 20, 56
first, 65
First Secretary, 67
First Secretary of the Georgian Communist
        Party, 18
Foreign Minister of the Soviet Union, 11, 18
Freedom of Assembly, 69
Freedom of Speech, 69
Freedom of the Press, 69
French, 9, 20, 30

Gelati, 49
General Secretary, 12
genocide, 53
Geocities, 75
George H. W. Bush, 70
George III of Imereti, 42
George Soros, 16
George X, 42
Georgia, 1, 2, 15, 27, 33, 35, 40, 41, 59, 65, 69
Georgia for the Georgians, 69
Georgian, 1, 5, 6, 9, 11, 12, 19, 21, 23, 27, 34,
        35, 41, 43, 45, 47, 49, 51, 55, 59,
        61, 63, 65
Georgian Academy of Sciences, 53
Georgian Communist Party, 12
Georgian history, 29

Georgian Orthodox, 34, 63
Georgian Orthodox and Apostolic Church, 24,
        31
Georgian Orthodox Christian, 33
Georgian Orthodox Church, 14, 20, 21, 28, 36,
        41, 43, 45, 47, 51, 52, 55, 56, 61,
        66
Georgian SSR, 40, 60, 65
Georgians, 15
German, 30, 36
Gestapo, 24
Giorgi Chanturia, 70
Giorgi Saakadze, 41
Giorgi X, 41
Giuseppe Garibaldi, 29
glasnost, 68
Goa, 36
Gori, 5, 6, 53, 55, 59
Gospels, 2
Gosudarstvennaya Duma, 30
Great Purge, 9, 12
Greece, 52, 63
Greek, 2, 63
Greek Orthodox, 24
Greek Orthodox Christianity, 51
Greeks, 64
grey, 12
Grozny, 73
Guria, 11, 19, 59
Gurjaani, 23

hegoumenos, 64
hegumen, 52
Helsinki Group, 66
Helsinki Watch, 69, 75
hierodeacon, 52
hieromonk, 52
Historical fiction, 27
History, 12
History of Georgia, 32
Holy Synod, 55
human chains, 53
Human Rights, 69
Human Rights Watch, 75
humanist, 27

Iberia, 30
Iberians, 64
Igor Ivanov, 15, 16
Ilia Chavchavadze, 42
Ilia II, 48
Ilia of Sukhumi and Abkhazia, 47
Ilori, 61
Imereti, 47
Imeretia, 59

Imperial Russia, 9, 19, 55, 59
Incumbent, 39, 51
independence, 31
independent Georgian church, 59
India, 36
Indiana University Press, 36
Interfax, 70
International Society for Human Rights, 66
invading Russian army, 60
Ioane, 64
Iran, 35
Isaak Brodskiy, 33
Islam, 35, 42
ISSN, 76
Istanbul, 2
Iviron, 64
Iviron Monastery, 63
IWPR, 16

Jerusalem, 52
Jewish, 34
Joseph Stalin, 5, 13, 20, 30, 31, 33
journalist, 27
Jumber Patiashvili, 18
jurist, 27

Kakheti, 23, 27–29, 35, 42
Kamenets-Podolsk, 56
Kamianets-Podilskyi, 56
Kardanakhi, 29
Kartli, 2, 41
Kashueti Church, 43, 52
katepano, 63
Kaunas, 56
Kazan, 42, 61
Ketevan Geladze, 5
KGB, 47
khan, 42
Kharagauli, 45
Khevi, 29
Kiev, 43, 55, 59
king, 41
king of Kakheti, 35
King of Kartli, 42
Kingdom of Imereti, 42
Komsomol, 12, 13
Konstantin Chernenko, 13
Konstantine Gamsakhurdia, 66
Kremlin, 12
ktetor, 64
Kutaisi, 21, 49, 55
Kvareli, 27, 28
Kvatakhevi Monastery, 56
Kyrion II, 59, 60

Lado Gurgenidze, 39
Lanchkhuti, 12
Lang, David M., 56
Lang, David Marshall, 37
language, 28
Lavra, 64
lawyer, 27
lb, 64
League of Nations, 20
Leeds University, 40
Leonid, 56
Leonid Brezhnev, 13, 67
liberal, 28
List of Georgians, 32
Lithuania, 56
locum tenens, 43
London, 56
Loti Kobalia, 73

M. Gaster, 2
Mamati, 11, 12
Maritsa, 2
Marseille, 20
martyr, 41
Marxist, 30
Medieval, 28
Melchizedek III, 44, 49, 50
Menachem Begin, 67
Mensheviks, 31
Menshevism, 12
mentor, 30
Merab Kostava, 13, 67
Metropolitan, 1
metropolitan, 43, 45, 52, 59
Mikhail Gorbachev, 12, 13, 68
Mikhail I, 42
Mikhail Saakashvili, 15, 74
Mikhail Sabinin, 41
Mikheil Saakashvili, 15, 32, 39, 53, 74
militiamen, 28
Mingrelia, 72
Mingrelian, 20
Minister of Foreign Affairs of the Soviet Union, 12
Ministry of External Affairs, Government of India, 36
Missal, 2
Mkhedrioni, 71, 72
monk, 49, 56
Moscow, 51–53
Most Holy Synod, 56
Mount Athos, 64
Mount Sinai, 2
Mt Athos, 63
Mtatsminda Pantheon, 74

Mtskheta, 27, 28, 30, 43, 47, 49, 52, 61
Mukhrani, 35

N.S., 41
Nanuli Shevardnadze, 11
Nanuli Tsagareishvili, 12
nation-building, 29
National revival, 32
NATO, 40
Nazi, 24
New York, 52
Nicholas Mavrocordatos, 2
Nik'oloz Baratashvili, 29
Nikita Khrushchev, 13
Nikozi, 55
Nino Burjanadze, 11, 15, 18
NKVD, 12
Noe Zhordania, 30
Normandy, 21
North Ossetia, 52
novelist, 27
NS, 1

O wi cim, 24
O.S., 27, 41
OCLC, 76
Odessa, 55
oil, 15
Okhrana, 31
Open Society Institute, 16
Organization, 12
Orgburo, 12
Orthodox, 21, 24
Orthodox Christian, 6, 40
Orthodox Christianity, 59
Orthodox Church in America, 42
Oscar Wilde, 66
Ossetia, 14
Ossetian, 5
Otpor, 16
Ottoman, 41
Ottoman Empire, 2

Pakistan, 70
palace, 34
Pankalia, 64
Paris, 20, 21
Parliament of Georgia, 15, 40
Pater Patriae, 28
patriarch, 64
patrikios, 63
patriotism, 49
Patrology, 24
patronymic, 75
Pennsylvania, 52

Persian, 41
Petritsoni Monastery, 24
Phanariote, 2
PhD, 23
philology, 66
philosopher, 1, 27
philosophy, 49
pipeline, 15
poet, 27
poetry, 29
Poland, 24
Polish, 30
Politburo, 12, 13
political asylum, 16
Political Imprisonment, 69
politician, 40
Polotsk, 56
polyglot, 6
Portuguese, 36
post-Soviet, 65
Poti, 73
Pravda, 13
President, 53, 65
President de Gaulle, 9
President of Georgia, 11, 18, 65, 77
priest, 34, 45
Prince, 2
printing press, 1
Protopope, 21
pseudonyms, 55
Pshav-Khevsureti, 28
psychiatry, 66
public domain, 2
publisher, 27
purge, 12

Râmnicu, 2
Ramzan Kadyrov, 74
Rayfield, Donald, 36
Realism, 27
referendum, 68
Refugee Law, 40
Republic of Cyprus, 40
Republic of Georgia, 2, 65
reunification, 16
Revue d'histoire ecclésiastique, 24
Romania, 1, 2, 24, 52, 70
Romanian, 1, 2
Romanian Orthodox Church, 1, 2
Rose Revolution, 12, 16, 32
Rostov-on-Don, 74
Routledge, 36
ruble, 6
rugby union, 2
Russia, 42, 51, 52

Russian, 5, 6, 9, 12, 27, 30, 34, 43, 55
Russian Civil War, 9
Russian counterpart, 43
Russian Duma, 30
Russian Empire, 5, 53, 61
Russian Orthodox Church, 49, 55, 56, 59
Russian-Georgian war, 53
Russification, 28
russification, 66

Safavid, 35
saint, 41
Saint Ilia the Righteous, 68
Saint Petersburg, 29
Samegrelo, 59, 72, 73
samizdat, 47, 66
scientist, 65
second President of Georgia, 12
Secretariat, 12
seminarian, 30
September 26, 36
Seraphim of Sarov, 21
serf, 6
serfs, 33
Sergei Bulgakov, 9
Sergey Kovalev, 66
Sergo Ordzhonikidze, 31
sermons, 2, 49
shah, 41
Shevardnadze, 73
Shiraz, 35, 42
Shota Rustaveli, 24, 66
Siberia, 67
Simon Sebag Montefiore, 7, 30–32, 34
Sinatra Doctrine, 13
Sioni Cathedral, 48
Slobodan Milo evi , 16
Society for the Spreading of Literacy Among
    Georgians, 30
South Ossetia, 40, 53, 69
South Ossetian Autonomous Oblast, 68
Soviet, 21, 43, 45, 47, 49, 52, 61, 66
Soviet Democratic Republic, 69
Soviet Peace Committee, 44
Soviet Union, 11, 12, 20, 65
St Petersburg, 56
St. Augustine, 36
St. John the Baptist, 59
St. Nino, 21
St. Petersburg, 9
St. Petersburg University, 19
St. Sergius Orthodox Theological Institute, 9,
    21
St. Tikhon's Orthodox Theological Seminary,
    52

St. Vladimir's Orthodox Theological Seminary,
    52
Stalin, 43, 66
state of emergency, 15
State of Israel, 40
Stechkin pistol, 73
Steny Hoyer, 70
strategos, 63
structure of the state, 12
Sukhumi, 61
Suny, Ronald Grigor, 36
Supreme Council of the Republic of Georgia, 68
Supreme Soviet, 12, 69
Svetitskhoveli Cathedral, 56
synkellos, 64
Synodal, 59

T. S. Eliot, 66
Tao-Klarjeti, 19
TASS, 67
Tbilisi, 2, 5, 15, 16, 19, 23, 31, 40, 41, 43,
    47–49, 52, 55, 59, 61, 65, 66, 74
Tbilisi Ilia Ch avch avadze State University Of
    Language and Culture, 32
Tbilisi Sioni Cathedral, 44, 49, 56, 61
Tbilisi State University, 20, 23, 40, 49
Tblisi, 14
Teimuraz I, 35
Teimuraz I of Kakheti, 42
Telavi, 6
Tengiz Kitovani, 70
Tengiz Sigua, 69
Tergi River, 29
The Guardian, 36
the International Herald Tribune, 53
The Iranian, 36
The Literature of Georgia: A History, 36
the Synod of the Romanian Orthodox Church, 1
Theologian, 51
theologian, 1, 23
Theology, 52
Tiflis, 6, 43, 45, 61
Tiflis Governorate, 55, 61
TIME Magazine, 17, 75
took orders, 2
Trans-Caspian region, 45
Transcaucasian SFSR, 11, 12
Transcaucasus, 15
Tsar, 42
tsar, 34
Tsarist autocracy, 30
Tsereteli, 31
Tsitsamuri, 27, 28
Tskhumi, 52
tuberculosis, 6

Tundzha, 2
Turkey, 15, 19, 70
Turkish, 6
tutelage, 2

Ukraine, 56, 70
Ukrainian, 30
Union of Citizens of Georgia, 11
United National Movement, 32
United States, 32
United States Congress, 67
University of Bonn, 24
University of Iowa, 75
University of Leipzig, 24
University of Paris, 9
University of St. Petersburg, Russia, 29
Urbnisi, 45
US Congressmen, 70

Vakhvakhishvili, 36
Vasil Mzhavanadze, 18
Vasily Mzhavanadze, 13
Velvet Revolution, 16
Vitebsk, 56
Vladikavkaz, 51, 52
Vladimir Lenin, 13
vote-rigging, 14

Wallachia, 1
Warsaw University, 24
was dispersed, 52
William Shakespeare, 66
World Council of Churches, 49, 52
World War II, 12, 20, 21, 31
writer, 27

Yugoslav, 16
Yuri Andropov, 13

Zugdidi, 20, 72
Zurab Noghaideli, 39
Zurab Zhvania, 15, 16
Zviad Gamsakhurdia, 11, 13, 14, 17, 18